You can follow my blog diaries at:
http://gingerbirdevans.wordpress.com

On twitter at:
http://twitter.com/gingerbirdevans

Facebook:
http://www.facebook.com/SexAndTheSignposts

Contact me at:
gingerbirdevans@hotmail.com

Sex and the Signposts
Gaynor Evans

ACKNOWLEDGEMENTS

I would like to thank everyone that has had to listen to me going on about this book for the last two years especially:

My wonderful children Laura, Kate, Rory and Jack for putting up with my dubious lifestyle and their continued support.

My very good friends Trudy, Tina, Jean, Josephine and Kriselda for picking up the pieces when things went wrong and for their love and encouragement.

My mate Amanda for giving me access to her wardrobe and flat and for leading the way.

Special thanks to Chloe for helping me with the technical stuff and Erica for the layout and Claire for the initial proof reading. Not forgetting Michelle for the great cover photo.

To Anna who gave me the final push I needed to get on with it!

Finally a big thank you to all the gorgeous Toyboys featured in these pages who enriched my life and made me feel whole again! With an affectionate nod to the Irish and Australian Flag.

Sex and the Signposts
Gaynor Evans

'We're here for a good time not a long time'

Sex and the Signposts
Gaynor Evans

PROLOGUE

I don't know why I started keeping a diary, except I remember the need to get organised and originally just kept it for arrangements and appointments. These of course, were mainly for Max, keeping track of his numerous hospital and doctors appointments, not to mention the ones for the solicitors who were fighting his court case.

We had embarked on suing the hospital for his failed back operations. I needed to have them in my diary because I went with him to most of them, in my role of the dutiful and supportive wife. I spent endless hours trawling through medical records and writing long and detailed emails to his solicitor. This was in addition to working full time (I was the breadwinner) running the home, sorting out the finances and supporting the children, not to mention walking the numerous dogs he had collected when he was too ill to manage and virtually worshipping the ground he walked on.

But then, as the storm clouds gathered over my marriage, I started scribbling about how I was feeling and found it a useful tool in coping with the day to day nightmare that my life had become. Relegated into the spare room on some pretence by my husband of eighteen years, accepting the insult because 'he was ill' and 'needed more space' I comforted myself with scrawling in the book and reading the whole collection of Harry Potter books one after the other. It was escapism at its best and boy did I need to escape!!

Writing the anecdotes in my diary just seemed to help. From my window I could see a huge pine tree in the woods beyond and I would stare at the tree for hours dreaming of the day when Max and I would be back on even ground. I found the view calming as it stood still and strong in all weathers, just like me I thought, it was a symbol of being resilient in the face of adversity. Ironic then, that when the marital home had to be sold for the divvy-up, the only view I could afford was the terraced house opposite and the local Co-operative.

Said husband of course would be surrounded by pine trees and views in his new life in the country. They say "you covet that which you see every day" and whilst I was coveting the pine tree he was coveting the woman who lived next door. This of course was the real reason I was seconded to the spare room and it would seem that the coveting had gone on for some years!

The discovery of this betrayal left me incandescent with rage. The rage, although directed firmly in his direction and also in the direction of "her next door" was partly turned in on myself. How could I have been so stupid as not to have known? Was I blind? Was I naïve? I berated myself for days, kicking myself all the way up the garden path that divided our two houses. Of course I was none of those

Sex and the Signposts
Gaynor Evans

things, but there is none as blind as those that cannot see and I couldn't see it even though it was right under my nose. I had had my suspicions and my woman's intuition had been telling me that there was something badly wrong, but they had been very, very clever.

My delightful husband never ever went out in the evenings. In the last five years and due to his repeated back operations he laid upstairs watching TV night after night and had only gone out a mere handful of times. How then had this affair been conducted and when? The answer was obvious, during the day, whilst I and her extremely hardworking husband were out earning a crust. (My husband was disabled out and she worked **very** part-time.) They must have been sharing lots of 'afternoon delight'. I must admit, I had wondered why he kept getting repeat prescriptions for Viagra, something he had been given ad lib due to his spinal damage. He certainly wasn't giving me the benefit of them but I was naively hoping he was stockpiling them to use with me at a later date or maybe selling them to his mates. God! How stupid was I? The amount of barefaced lies he must have told me should be recorded in the Guinness Book of Records.

The revelations left me on my knees. I ranted when he told me he was going off to his new country life with her (something I'd always dreamed about, and I still to this day cannot watch the TV show 'Escape

Sex and the Signposts
Gaynor Evans

to the Country') I screamed when he told me that it had been going on for over five years. I fought with him and I slapped her and then I felt a great deal better.

Once the storm had subsided I drew a sharp intake of breath and evaluated my position. So this was it! I was going to be on my own, a middle aged woman, loyal wife for eighteen years through lots of sickness and not much health. Thrown on the rubbish heap of singledom, alone and bloody terrified! I gave myself a good talking to and decided that this terrible betrayal was not going to beat me. Quoting to myself an adage that I'd read somewhere "It's not what life throws at you, it's how you handle it that counts". I decided that I was not only going to handle it I was going to wrestle it into submission.

Resplendent in a red dress, with high heels to match, and glass of champagne in hand, I supervised his removal from my life and into the waiting van. I asked sarcastically "Now have you got everything?" His response was a steely glare. I smiled sipping my champagne as the leather chesterfield that he had humbly asked if he could take left the house and giggled loudly as it was loaded onto the van. I had been kind enough to buy him and his new squeeze a house warming present. It was a hot June day and the 'present' should be warming nicely in the springs of the family chesterfield. I wonder how long it will take them to

Sex and the Signposts
Gaynor Evans

find that nice piece of haddock?

The thought of it rotting away and them franticly trying to find the source of the smell gave me a great deal of comfort in the days that followed as did the arms of a rather gorgeous toyboy or two. Now this is where my diary entries become much more interesting.

Sex and the Signposts
Gaynor Evans

CONTENTS

1 Vomit and Vino
2 The Mrs Robinson Effect
3 Horses Hats and Hotties
4 Coitus Interruptus
5 Radio Active Romance
6 Brains Brawn and Bourguignon
7 Waltzing Matilda
8 Sex and Signposts
9 Catch 22
10 Confused.com
11 The Irish Eyes are smiling
12 Hotter than My Daughter
13 Jumping Jack Flash
14 Feeling the Fear
15 Pocket Size Perfection
16 Danny Boy
17 Frustrations and Eruptions
18 Fitness First
19 Patience is a Virtue
20 Babes in Banus
21 Cinderella and the NOT So Charming Prince
22 Concluding the Cougar

Sex and the Signposts
Gaynor Evans

Chapter One
VOMIT AND VINO

Finding the underwear receipt under the bed had been rather cathartic. I knew there was someone else, but I hadn't been able to gather the evidence, my husband having put up so many smokescreens, I had been blinded, BUT I just knew! I was always checking his room, sniffing around like a bloodhound looking for anything to indicate what he was up to. Now I had found something tangible - at last!

Quickly, checking over the size, 34C bra, and size 12 thong La Senza winter flock design - aaw how sweet! The question is who did it fit? There were two women under suspicion. Her who lived next door or the woman he walked the dogs with? Getting a mental picture in my head of both women, I sat on the edge of the bed and turning the receipt over in my hand, I made a choice it was definitely her next door. Whoopee! At last I could now see what I'd been feeling for months.

Carefully, replacing it in exactly the same place under the bed, I left the room smiling to myself. Sherlock Holmes had nothing on me. Now what to do with the information? As it was our son's seventeenth birthday and he was having some friends stay for a sleepover my husband had decided to duck out. Heaven forbid that he should stick around to help clear up after seven gangly

Sex and the Signposts
Gaynor Evans

teenagers. As always, it was left to me to deal with the sharp end and he had taken himself off for the weekend.

I decided that, for now, I would keep my discovery to myself. Revenge is a dish best served cold and I needed a game plan. Talking of games, I also had a date that evening. He wasn't the only one that could find solace in the arms of another, so there! I was going over to an old friend/flame's house for dinner. We had known each other for years and had dated a little, way back when, and there had been a bit of a spark, and as his wife had left him the year before, we had been out for dinner recently.

I wasn't sure whether the spark was still alight and would rise like a phoenix from the ashes or whether we were, in fact, just good friends. I knew his expectation at the end of this evening would be to take me to bed and I had decided to give it a try. About time I thought, although I was a bit rusty and certainly more than a bit nervous as I hadn't had that many sexual partners. But fired up with the evidence of my husband's infidelity a bit of revenge sex is just what the doctor ordered. My husband knew this man quite well and would hate the thought of it. That alone made it much more tempting. Plus he had his own business and a nice house and at least wanted to get my knickers off.

Being a responsible parent, my intention was to be out quite late but to come home to make sure that

Sex and the Signposts
Gaynor Evans

the boys didn't set fire to the house or terrorise the neighbours. Although I secretly hoped they would make loads of noise and keep a certain neighbour awake!!

So dressed up to the nines I was delivered, by my daughter, to my date's house and he had kindly agreed to drop me home at my convenience. We had spoken briefly on the phone and I had explained the reasons why I had to come home. He was fine about it although I got the impression he wanted us to have a sleepover of our own. Of course what he actually meant was that he wanted to take me to bed. I played my part and implied that I might be the dessert. I asked if I should bring anything like wine but he said he had plenty, although of course, he was on the wagon.

In our earlier life he had been a big drinker and had now given up. I remember thinking he was more fun as a drunk but it was a lifestyle choice as he had been ill recently. His lovely cottage was out in the sticks it was beautifully decorated and well located. The man could be quite a catch, if I was an opportunist.

He welcomed me in and the smell of something good cooking in the oven wafted under my nose. My problem was that the revelations of the day had somewhat dulled my appetite, plus I was nervous and the two things combined seemed to have filled up the space where my stomach used to be.

Sex and the Signposts
Gaynor Evans

He had gone to a lot of trouble, beautifully marinated and slow cooked lamb shanks, and lots of fresh vegetables. Nothing else for it, I would just have to get drunk. He offered me wine and I said yes please. Unfortunately, the lots of wine he had told me about were all of the white variety. My stomach and I prefer red, but beggars can't be choosers, so glass in hand I started slugging it back. Glass one: to make me stop getting a mental picture of 'her next door' in the 'winter flock' design. Glass two: to settle my nerves. Glass three: to help the food go down and Glass four: because I'd forgotten I'd drunk the other three!

My host sat drinking a glass of water opposite me and seemed a little subdued and then proceeded to tell me how his last romance went tits up, time for glass five. I forced as much food down as I could and we left the table and retired to the TV room where we sat side by side on his seduction sofa. I imagine that the sofa had been utilised this way many times before.

He had kindly opened another bottle of wine for me so my glass seemed to be full again ... oh well it would be rude not to drink it so down went glass six. He was still on water and there we sat, him talking and me slurring in front of one of the biggest flat screen TV's I'd ever seen. Halfway through glass seven the kissing started. By now I was more than three parts to the wind and knew that the bedroom was beckoning. He was keen, eager and sober - I was just sozzled. "Shall we go to bed?" he said, almost straight away. Ah! the foreplay was over then!

Accepting my fate, although incapable of feeling much at all, I nodded in agreement and he made for the stairs. I excused myself to the bathroom and tried to get my head together while I peed. God I really was drunk - this was not good! I had a man upstairs who had waited over twenty years to get me naked and here I am barely able to stand, let alone perform acrobatics in the bedroom. I also had the nagging worry of how the boys were doing back at home. I wonder if they had managed to stay sober, unlike me. I think I knew the answer. But back to the job in hand!

Getting off the toilet seat, I did at least remember to wipe myself thoroughly. I daresay he would want an excursion into the undergrowth. Kicking of my shoes so I didn't break my neck, I climbed the stairs. He was already in bed, naked as the day he was born. He watched me undress and then saying to myself "right, I'm going in" I jumped in and snuggled under the covers.

The sex is a hazy memory, we did all the usual things, I think!! He seemed to enjoy himself, I don't know if I did, but seven glasses of wine will do that to you. I had decided beforehand that falling asleep wouldn't be a good idea for two reasons. One was that I had to go home, and two;

Sex and the Signposts
Gaynor Evans

there was my snoring to consider. According to my husband, my snoring is so bad that I sound like a warthog. This is not something you want to do when you are trying to impress a new man. I had sort of mentioned it earlier but still. Trying not to fall asleep sounds so easy but when you have consumed a bottle and a half of wine, it's damn near impossible. Anyway I didn't fall asleep, I just passed out!

I came round with a start a few hours later. At first I didn't know why I was awake or where I was. He was sleeping deeply beside me and grabbing for my phone I checked the time - 2.30am - bloody hell! God knows what state my house was going to be in. I had to get home. I started searching for my clothes and then I realised what had woken me. I felt sick, really sick.

By now my bed companion was stirring and I said I needed to get home. He wasn't overjoyed at having to leave his cosy bed and go out into the cold and drive me home but being a man of his word he got up and got dressed. He then proceeded to tell me that I did snore and yes it was quite loud. Oh great! I'm never sleeping with a man again! I bent down to put on my shoes, with my head spinning and the sickness rising.

The nausea was getting worse and the need to chuck up the wine and lamb shanks was all I could think about. But I can't, I thought. It's bad enough that I

Sex and the Signposts
Gaynor Evans

got drunk with someone who has taken the pledge, passed out in the bedroom and then snored so loudly he felt he had to mention it, and now I'm dragging him out of bed to take me home. Throwing up would be the final insult, he'd either think it was his cooking, or worse still the sex. No! No! I can't do it. Swallowing down the contents of my stomach with every intake of breath, I climbed in his car and he drove me home.

Luckily it wasn't far but every mile was murder, as the nausea got worse once the car was in motion. I made small talk in between reciting over and over to myself "don't be sick", "don't be sick". We pulled up outside my house, which although still standing was lit up like a Christmas tree. Leaning in for a quick peck on the cheek, I said thanks for a lovely evening and climbed out of the car, walking as straight as I could towards the house. The relief at getting home filtered through to my stomach and unable to suppress the waves of nausea anymore, I started heaving. Looking back, I saw he was still sitting there making sure I got in safely. A real gentleman, but I wish he'd bloody well go! I didn't want him to see me heaving as I negotiated my way up the steps.

I waved and watched him drive off and now running up the drive, I got as far as the back gate and unable to hold it down anymore, I threw up the whole contents of my stomach, all over the garden. The security light alerted to my presence clicked on,

Sex and the Signposts
Gaynor Evans

setting off the dogs, and I was under the spotlight. Shining brightly and glistening in the light were the remnants of the lamb shanks mixed in with peas, mange tout, and of course carrots - there for the entire world to see. Straightening up, and wiping my mouth on my arm, I took a deep breath and then went through the back door where I was greeted by vomit in the sink, one boy passed out in the fireplace, two more on the floor and the reek of beer everywhere. Shouting up the stairs to my son, mustering as much indignation as possible, I said "who's been sick in my sink?" Oh the irony.

I made a mental note to clear up my own vomit in the morning and checking that each boy was in the recovery position, and warm enough, I crawled into bed. I awoke quite early and long before the boys, who seem to be able to sleep though anything. I now had a good opportunity to clear away my disgraceful evidence. I mixed up some disinfectant, and armed with a broom, I went to the back gate. There was absolutely no sign of it. The smell was still lingering but there was no trace of any sick. I stood there for a moment puzzled, trying to work out where it had gone; and then I realised, one of the dogs had eaten it! Talk about recycling! Ah well, perhaps the whole experience was a sign that I should let sleeping dogs lie for now and keep my knickers up and my food down…at least till my divorce.

Sex and the Signposts
Gaynor Evans

Chapter Two
THE MRS ROBINSON EFFECT

I opened my diary and staring at the date, 10 June 2008, I raised my pen and just for a moment I couldn't bring myself to write the words 'Max leaves today'. There it was in black and white and finally it was over. The long and protracted death of my marriage draws to a close. I didn't know how to feel. At first a sense of relief was followed by a rush of excitement or was it fear of the unknown? Being on my own without a man in tow was not something I was used to and especially hard to face at my age! Refusing to let myself dwell on his departure, I threw a 'Divorce Party' a strictly all girl affair. I announced it on my Facebook page for the following evening. I prepared some food and everyone brought a bottle.

My house and garden was full to the brim with friends, old and new, that came to lend their support. They knew I had been through a lot and enjoying the warm summer's evening we exchanged stories about life, loves and the future. Nothing like a bit of girl power to blow away all traces of a man and with much giggling about the hidden haddock, the whole evening was a great success and with my annual visit to the Ascot Races on the horizon I was in a buoyant mood.

Later that week, I was in a local pub having a noisy and hilarious conversation with anyone that would

Sex and the Signposts
Gaynor Evans

listen when I announced loudly that "All I need now is a nice toyboy". A young guy that I knew vaguely shouted back "look no further". I turned to look at him and thought "hmmm nice but young". He grinned at me our eyes met and I could feel a stirring. Deciding that he was joking I made a quick exit. But it didn't end there.

Over the next few weeks we bumped into each other a few times. I found out his name was Jason. We had some mutual acquaintances and spent lazy hours in various pub gardens, chatting about this and that and making small talk. I was just happy to be out and about and wanted to enjoy my new found freedom. I still had the moving to do but that, as usual, was stuck in the legalities. So I was happy to be diverted and he certainly diverted me. Always pleased to see me, his face would light up when I arrived anywhere. He was light and easy company and very easy on the eye. Tall, at least 6ft 3, he had a mop of blonde hair and large expressive blue eyes. He was all arms and legs and rather on the lean side but I didn't mind that, lean and keen I thought.

At some point we exchanged mobile numbers and we used to text each other from time to time. He was growing on me, but I just wasn't sure he was serious or that I should, after all he was only twenty and it seemed too shocking to contemplate. I wrestled with the rights and wrongs of taking it any further but the temptation was getting more difficult to resist. I was keen to find my feet and I felt the

Sex and the Signposts
Gaynor Evans

need to establish myself as a single, confident woman with a sex life. There had been precious little sex in the last two years of my marriage and as I rated sex highly on my 'To do' list, I had missed it in more ways than one. Painful as my first attempt at filling the gap had been and resulting in the hangover from hell, freedom gained, I was now chomping at the bit. So, his obvious interest in me sexually, he kept those blue eyes of his trained permanently on my cleavage, was quite intoxicating and I found myself flirting quite openly with him, just to test the water. The water soon reached boiling point.

One warm balmy summers evening (16th July according to my diary) a few of us were meeting at the local pub after work. He was there as usual and we exchanged a few words and glances. My intention was to have just one white wine spritzer, but the conversation was fun and before I knew it we were on number three. He manoeuvred himself so he was sitting next to me and suddenly my phone went off indicating I had a message. I opened the message; it was from him, three simple words "I want you". My stomach did a summersault and looking at him I whispered "If we do this, no one, and I mean **no one**, is to know". He nodded vigorously in my direction but I got the impression he would have agreed to jump off a cliff if I'd told him too. The fact that we had to be so covert made the whole thing more exciting and very naughty. So decision made the next problem was where?

Sex and the Signposts
Gaynor Evans

My son was at home most of the time and he lived with relatives. I was suddenly feeling exceedingly rampant and my mind was racing, trying to think of somewhere we could go. The daily HRT was working a treat and having been celibate for months my desire was taking over any idea that my brain might have had on being sensible. He wanted me and that in itself is a big turn on. In my head I was already conjuring up pictures of the kissing and the stroking and the getting naked. At this point one of the crowd suggested we went back to her place so we fell out of the pub and chattering loudly we made our way there.

Jason and I acted quite normally but exchanged deep and meaningful glances, which had the effect of revving up my already simmering lust. And then, as luck would have it, we found ourselves alone in the hallway. At last, an opportunity. Talking about something totally irrelevant just to keep up the pretence, we edged closer and closer until, whilst pretending to admire a photo on the wall, we managed a furtive but passionate kiss. My revving turned into a full blown engine roar and blowing caution to the wind I suggested that I could possibly sneak him in at home, if he was game. Indicating that even if he wasn't game, the thing in his trousers was definitely rising to the occasion. We fashioned a plan of escape. He was to appear to go home and then double back and arrive on my doorstep. We spun our stories and made our excuses. He was getting dropped off by a friend and I was on foot, they drove past me and I waved them off giggling all the way home.

Luckily my son was asleep and as the house was quite big and he slept on one side and me on the other, I figured that, with a bit of luck, I could get away with this and he need never know. I slipped into a silky dressing gown but left my bra and knickers on to make me feel less naked. Then the panic set in. Oh My God! Was I mad? I was about to have sex with a boy young enough to be my son's mate (he wasn't!) I wish I'd been on the diet longer; hope I can have the light off; would he notice my back fat; did I smell alright; Oh Christ did the bed squeak? I ran over and gave it a wiggle.

The only action this bed had seen was me in it alone, sleeping, snoring and reading 'Harry Potter ' and Dr. Phil's 'Relationship Rescue' - fat lot of good that was! The bed was a virgin and I bloody felt like one. Just at the point where I was losing my nerve, I saw the security light go on and looking down I could see his tall gangly figure lurking on the steps below.

I crept down the landing listening at my son's door for any movement on the way. My biggest nightmare would be for my son to discover me in the throes of passion and yet I was still prepared to take the chance. Funny thing desire, it makes you takes risks. Opening the door and ushering him in, I lead him up the stairs, like a lamb to the slaughter!

Sex and the Signposts
Gaynor Evans

Past my son's room, and onto my side of the house. Once inside, with the door firmly shut, I felt a little better. It was rare for my son to wake. Please god, don't let it be tonight.

Once alone he seemed a little nervous and I now seemed to be in charge. Suggesting he may want to get into the bed he undressed and, leaving his pants on, slipped under the covers. I had a glimpse of his body and as I imagined, he was very wiry and looked like he needed a decent meal. Handy then that he was about to have me on a plate. I stood in front of him and slipped off my dressing gown, trying to be seductive.

I had turned off the light but the room was illuminated by the street lights and the full moon that had risen - not an omen I hope! The sight of my body seemed to excite him and he muttered something about "gorgeous and sexy" as I slipped in beside him. We kissed and kissed and then kissed some more. He still seemed a little anxious and excitable but was exploring my body with enthusiasm. In fact, it was like going to bed with an adorable puppy. He loved everything, my boobs, and my fats bits and as he worked his way down I remember thinking I hope he's into ginger hair. It seemed he was and he spent ages paying homage to it with his tongue and fingers. I was exhilarated, excited and really enjoying myself. I stroked and played with his erection and couldn't wait to have it inside me. When the moment came I was beyond ready. Maintaining eye contact the whole time he climbed aboard, reaching down I grabbed his cock and guided it inside me.

Oh! God how I'd missed this feeling, it was like coming home. He moved slowly within me then faster and faster, in between he stroked my breasts and kissed me hard. It went on and on and I remember thinking that the boy had some stamina. We changed position once, I would have got on top but I remember reading that older woman should never assume that position as everything hangs downwards and looks awful. So that was a big 'no no'. I was reaching the point of exhaustion when he whispered to me softly "where would you like me to come?" I was bemused. Was it a trick question? No one had ever asked me that before. Thinking it was some new sexual etiquette that I wasn't aware of, I mumbled "Erm, well I thought that it was obvious, inside me please, soon as your ready". No chance of pregnancy here sunshine, I whispered inwardly.

This seemed to excite him further and unable to contain himself anymore, he did as he was told, groaning loudly. He flopped back in the bed saying "that was wicked" and I was instantly reminded of how young he was. I had actually forgotten for a while. We cuddled up and fell asleep, until waking with a start and checking the time, it was nearly four o'clock. I roused him and told him he had to go. Passion spent, my sensible head was back on

Sex and the Signposts
Gaynor Evans

and it was imperative that my son didn't see him.

Reluctantly, he left the warmth of the bed and put his clothes on. I slipped into the silky dressing gown and took him to the front door. We kissed briefly and I repeated my mantra of "no one must know". I climbed back into the newly 'christened' bed and I was soon asleep. In the morning, I re-ran the evening over and over in my head singing to myself "bad girl, bad girl, naughty, naughty, bad girl". Then grabbing my phone, I sent him a text.

"Age is strictly a case of mind over matter! If you don't mind it doesn't matter"

Sex and the Signposts
Gaynor Evans

Chapter Three
HORSES, HATS & HOTTIES

One of the biggest days in my diary is my annual visit to Ascot races. To say I love it would be an understatement. I revel in the build-up, team discussions of whose wearing what the frantic shopping expeditions into London for "The" dress and the visits to the Beauty salon for preening pruning and the inevitable spray tan. I organise the food to soak up the copious amounts of alcohol that will be consumed by 'Team Gaynor'. The girls look forward to the newsletter that I send out with jokes about previous years and instructions on where to come, at what time and what to bring. The anticipation is huge.

I've been going for a number years but the day took on more importance with the demise of my marriage. The main reason for this is that the place is brimming with gorgeous sexy men. They are all suited and booted and smell divine and are in large rowdy groups, where the competitive edge takes over and you can virtually smell the testosterone. It's rather like a whole day of speed dating and providing you can stay upright on your stilettos the chances are you will meet some pretty hot guys. If it's a nice warm day then the atmosphere is electric from the ridiculously priced champagne corks popping one after another to the sound of the horses pounding round the track. The chance of a glimpse of the Royal family in the usual pomp and

Sex and the Signposts
Gaynor Evans

circumstance makes it an occasion to remember. It's heady and intoxicating and the women all beautifully turned out mill around chatting to each other and any available male that happens to stray into their path. Fuelled with champagne it becomes easy to fall into conversation all of which will be promptly forgotten.

The first time I got the 'Ascot' bug was when my marriage was just hanging by a thread, I found myself talking to a young man of thirty. We struck up conversation whilst cheering on the horses and he asked me to go for a drink with him Thinking he was just being friendly, I toddled off holding his hand, feeling all girlie as he lead me to the bar. He plied me with a large gin and tonic. Frankly there was no need to ply me with anything; I'd already drunk a whole bottle of champers! I remember thinking bloody hell!!! What am I doing? married woman and all that but I loved the attention he was giving me. Plus as far as I was concerned he couldn't possibly be interested in me in the real sense of the word, I was far too old. When things got a bit cosy and we were pushed together by the hoards of people vying for a place at the bar, he used the up close and personal proximity we found ourselves to kiss me. I was shocked, but was too polite to draw back and I quite liked it. It was years since I had been kissed by a stranger. When he asked for my number I gave it to him without hesitating, I was feeling totally reckless by now.

Sex and the Signposts
Gaynor Evans

We went back to our respective groups of friends and he text me later saying he would like to see me again and that I was gorgeous. I kept looking at the text in disbelief, bearing in mind that this was some years ago, long before the 'Cougar' thing was fashionable I have to say I was flattered and pleased that I still had it!! Well some of it anyway!! My husband had made it quite clear that he didn't think I came into the gorgeous category being preoccupied with his own troubles and of course he was already servicing the filly next door (although I didn't know it then). So I came back from Ascot head held high having had a thoroughly enjoyable day. Hungover of course, but happy. That was it, I was hooked. I did feel very uncomfortable whenever. I thought of the kiss and despite the fact he did text me after the event to ask me out, I refused. I was still living in hope that my marriage was going to stay the course and I wasn't going to do anything to jeopardize that. It wouldn't be fair to cheat on my poorly husband even though he was becoming increasingly more difficult to live with. He deserved better than that, or so I thought.

The next year arrived June 18th 2008 and I had been single for all of ten days. With the bottles of champers chilling in the fridge, I got ready stepping into my black and cream dress fascinator in place. I welcomed the girls as they arrived and there was much air kissing and complimentary noises being made. All fourteen of us looked fabulous and we set off in two cars with the champagne already opened

Sex and the Signposts
Gaynor Evans

and being drunk.

Phil is our regular driver and is used to dealing with us when our behaviour gets less than lady like (which is more often than not!) Everyone stores his number in their phone and then if you get lost or in difficulty he will come and find you and escort you back to the car. Trying to find your way back to base camp can be quite difficult if you wander off as all the car parks look the same and the fact that you have drunk at least a whole bottle of champagne, means your judgment is well off. Your feet hurt and your fascinator and you are both tipsy. So Phil is like our personal minder and a great asset.

Rhianna's song 'Under my umbrella' is being played a lot on the radio as we wing our way to Windsor. Very appropriate as the weather is not the best and is overcast and rain is forecast. I had instructed all the 'ladies' to bring an umbrella. Mine proved very useful as I was to be joined under it by a hot young man of twenty five during a down pour. I decided that when numbers were exchanged and the texts started flying back and forth, that this time I would not miss the opportunity to see him again. I had already "pulled" a guy in his late thirties and we had chatted and had a bit of a kiss earlier in the day. I was still standing with him when I put up my umbrella to shield me from the rain. Nothing worse than rain to spoil your hair and make you look like a drowned rat. Taking absolutely no notice of the fact that I was already ahem! spoken for, the cheeky

Sex and the Signposts
Gaynor Evans

twenty five year old just stuck his head in and proceeded to chat me up in double quick time.

The other guy just sort of faded into the crowd and I was left being hit upon in no uncertain terms by this charming man. His name was Anthony and he worked for an online betting company. Talking at an alarming rate he told me he was into older women and could he have my number? I was so sexy and did I like younger guys? Before I could answer all of his questions he was snogging my face off. Oops! Two men in one day now that is bad. Anthony had big brown eyes and dark hair and most importantly a lovely smile and nice teeth. I rate nice teeth as high on my wish list where men are concerned and shy away from a bad set. I was intrigued and flattered so when he suggested we meet up in the fields outside I was quite taken with the idea. But despite talking to each other on our mobiles on the way back to the cars I couldn't for the life of me find him. I had champagne legs and they were just not working properly.

So when he text me later I was pleased and winged back an immediate reply. The texts flew back and forth for a few days with his ones getting more explicit followed early one Monday morning by a shocking picture of his 'morning glory' with the words "Come and sit on this". Spluttering my tea all over the place and laughing my head off, I replied with "Chance would be a fine thing"

Sex and the Signposts
Gaynor Evans

He was constantly urging me to get train to Surrey and book a hotel for a night of passion. I was far too chicken to contemplate such a thing. So our cyber sex continued. He phoned me one night and obviously wanted me to have sex with him over the airwaves. Having absolutely no idea what to say I blundered along talking about what underwear I had on (I lied of course) and moaning appropriately when I had ran out of ideas. I didn't have a clue, when I was younger the nearest thing we had to phone sex was blowing the odd kiss into the mouthpiece. That and the fact there were no mobiles just one big giant phone planted on the hall table and in full earshot of your mum and dad, talking dirty was not something I had learnt to do. The invention of the mobile had certainly changed the world.

He was very keen to meet up again but the distance was proving to be an issue. One Tuesday in late July the texting was full of sexual innuendo. I was beginning to get the hang of sex texting and he was getting very excited at the other end. Mentioning that I had possession of my friends empty flat that night he suddenly said that he had decided to drive over to see me, saying "I can't wait anymore and if we don't do it soon it won't happen". Not believing he was serious as he was in Central London today and the drive to me would be horrendous. I laboured the point. He would not be dissuaded. Asking for the postcode he did a check on the net and said he would be with me in a few hours.

Sex and the Signposts
Gaynor Evans

I still did not quite believe that he was actually coming. I worked through the rest of the afternoon and when he text me to say he was an hour away I decided I'd better get ready. I went quickly to the flat and got prepared for what I expected was going to be a raunchy couple of hours. Legs shaved check! Nice underwear on check! Make-up good check! Perfume sprayed! Check! Wine chilling! Check. Just as he was due to arrive all the lights went out! and the TV, and the stereo in fact everything! Great!!! It seems were in the throes of a power cut. Panicking I thought what can I do?

It dawned on me that I wouldn't be able to play any mood enhancing music and although the light was ok at the moment it was an overcast day so it would fade pretty rapidly. I had no idea how long they would take to restore the power. But from previous experience it could well be a few hours. I would just have to make contingency plans. Grabbing my purse I legged it, well tottered I was wearing my best heels, down the road to the Co-operative, I might bemoan the view of it, but it was proving to be a very useful place. I swooped on a big bag of T light candles. They would have to do. Rushing back to the flat which was already stooped in gloom, I strategically placed them around the lounge and then lit them one by one. I was getting exceedingly nervous now and excited, so I poured myself a large glass of wine. I knocked half of it back and it rushed into my empty stomach with immediate effect. Thank god for that at least I felt a bit calmer and the

Sex and the Signposts
Gaynor Evans

candles gave the room a nice rosy glow and hopefully would do the same for me.

I was ever anxious that my not so young and rather well covered body would send some young man running for the hills at some point. This young man it would seem would not be the one. He rang to say he was outside and I nervously opened the door it had been some weeks since I had seen him and I hoped I still liked the look of him and he of me. He grinned broadly and before I could get a good look at him he scooped me up off my feet and kissed me with passion. Putting me down again I had a chance to look at him clearly, well as clearly as I could, given the candlelight. I was talking nineteen to the dozen and offering him a beer and filling up my glass again I quickly explained the reason for the candles. He was as I remembered, quite tall and very broad and well built, a mop of brown hair and big wide apart brown eyes and with a huge smile revealing a perfectly formed line of choppers. He had a cheeky face and a cheeky manner to match but the chemistry was definitely there and it was working its magic.

We had only been talking for ten minutes when he grabbed me again and kissing me with meaning and reminding me of his tongue he started to undo the buttons on my shirt and pulling up my skirt. Pulling his t-shirt over his head, he then started undoing his trousers. He was not giving me a chance to object and was very much in charge. Dropping his trousers

Sex and the Signposts
Gaynor Evans

and pants to the floor and stepping out of them he allowed his cock to roam free stroking it as he did so, so that I could get the full benefit. It was rather big and very long!! I took a deep intake of breath savouring the moment as with his huge brown eyes fixed on me and darkening with lust he tried to wrestle me out of my bra. He decided to leave it in place but managed to extract my breasts from there resting place. "Mmmm" he said "you have great tits!!!" and playing with my left nipple with one hand he produced his mobile from his pocket with the other and showed me a picture of him and me at Ascot together. I don't remember that being taken! But there we were deep in conversation under my umbrella. How sweet that he had kept it.

Pushing me gently downward to my knees he made it quite clear what was expected next. It was a new experience for me to be so out of control but I rather liked it. I gazed up at him wide-eyed and then took his extensive manhood in my mouth which was rather a feat. Surprisingly, I managed quite well and without gagging and was really getting into this experience. I was already imagining what it was going to feel like inside me and hoped it would fit. I didn't have to wait long...we were still in the lounge and the rest of the flat was steeped in darkness. Deciding that he didn't want to go to the bedroom and still taking charge, he pulled me over to the dining table and scooping everything off in one movement, he lifted me up and laid me down. It was just like a scene from the film 'The Postman

Sex and the Signposts
Gaynor Evans

Only Rings Twice'. He may not be Jack Nicholson but he was certainly acting the part. Everything was happening very fast and my heart was pounding as coming level with the table he yanked me further to the edge and then taking his now rock hard erection in his hand he hovered for a minute letting my anticipation build before he rammed it hard and quickly inside me. I let out a huge moan and he drove in and out of me fast and strong.

I was still wearing my skirt and shoes, my thong he had just moved to one side. But it didn't matter. It felt good, really good and I was moaning loudly. He was really enjoying his work...and I lifted myself up onto my elbows so I could kiss him here and there. It was hard though, he was pushing inside with such force I couldn't maintain the lift and repeatedly collapsed back onto the table. Suddenly he pulled me up and with a great sense of urgency he turned me around letting my feet rest on the floor and with me leaning on the table for support he slide right back in. He was moaning loudly now and I was trying to control myself vocally, but it was hard given the size of the man (boy). I had totally abandoned myself to this guy and I was loving it, I don't ever remember being so out of control. Suddenly he announced that he was coming. And gasping loudly he did!

I remained in the prose position gasping for breath he was regaining his composure and eventually he slipped out of me leaving me feeling empty. I

Sex and the Signposts
Gaynor Evans

turned round to face him and we smiled warmly at each and kissed briefly. Adjusting my clothes I offered him another drink and he started to get dressed. We sat in the candle light chatting away and sipping our drinks, getting to know each other a little better, ironic really considering our bodies had been introduced first. It was getting late and he had quite a journey ahead of him and he said "I'd better go soon". I answered "yes of course" but somewhere during the chat our eyes locked and the chemistry that had been happily satiated suddenly started to rear up again. I felt it and so did he. Slowly putting his glass down he said quietly "I'd better go" "Ok" I said rising to my feet. "But first" he replied pausing for effect "I think we should do that all again". I blinked looking at him with disbelief "are you serious"? "Yep" he answered confidently and taking me by the hand he took me back to the table. I gulped!

He took off all his clothes in a flash and before I knew it there it was again huge and hard and inside me. "Oh My God" .I was almost overwhelmed and he was insatiable. But never the less it was just as amazing the second time and he was able to go on for much longer. I wanted to take control and asked him to lie on the floor deciding it was time to ride my Ascot Stallion. It was quite a daunting prospect as I lowered myself down, and it took a few attempts to ease him in, he was such a "big boy" I was still half dressed but he took the opportunity to play with my breasts and suck my nipples. I thanked

Sex and the Signposts
Gaynor Evans

god that my thighs were in good shape and I was able to keep up the pace. Eventually we were both over the finish line and frankly I couldn't have gone on much longer and would have had to pull him up. One thing I hadn't thought about was the hardness of the carpet and as I stood up I realised I had two nasty carpet burns. Ouch! I hadn't sported a sex related injury since my teens and these were going to be a dead giveaway.

We gathered ourselves together as my phone went off. I checked it was my son just seeing what time I would be home. I sent back "soon" and showed my young lover to the door. Kissing him and saying our goodbyes he went on his way. He phoned me a couple of times for directions and it took him over two hours to get home. Blowing out the candles I collected my stuff and made for the door, just as I did the lights came back on, along with the TV and the stereo. Laughing I went round turning everything off. Sex by candlelight had been exhilarating, so thanks Powergen! My thighs having received a thorough work out felt wobbly and I was walking like Id spent a day in the saddle. I was relieved to get home and flop on the sofa.

I lay there going over the events of the evening. I had never been overly adventurous sexually, and liked all the usual things but realized that night that I had the capacity to be a real sexual diva. I liked the feeling of being out of control, I liked the fact that it was sex without real emotions being involved and I loved the fact that twenty five years olds can go on forever. Hmmm, I was beginning to enjoy the single life and I never thought I would hear myself say that so soon. I was relishing in the fact that I answered to no one but me and could do what I liked, when I liked. I had no man demanding my attention. I could lay on this sofa all night if I chose to without requests for this or that. It was sheer bliss and being free was proving to be an uplifting experience and not the dark lonely one that I was expecting to have. I thought to myself that there was a lot to be said for being 'The older woman' Falling into a deep sleep I woke up some hours later with a contented smile on my face.

NB:
Although we are still in touch, Anthony and I have never managed to find each other at Ascot or meet up again. But never say never! My knees took ages to heal and the scars are still visible, that will teach me!

Sex and the Signposts
Gaynor Evans

Chapter Four
COITUS INTERRUPTUS

I always looked forward to my Friday nights out. By Friday night, I was ready to let my hair down and relax into the weekend. Sometimes my over-full weeks would wear me out both mentally and physically, either way a good night out would lift the spirits and get the weekend off to a fine start. As usual, the preening, pruning and titivation would start early and of course a glass of wine would be sipped constantly every step of the way, with the music blaring away to set the mood. Getting ready was a bit of an arduous task.

I had always been big on make-up. When I was sixteen a night out would take two hours of preparation. Getting the face ready in those days was quite a work of art. Three different eye shadows, false eyelashes stuck carefully on, usually top and bottom and, if not, you meticulously painted the lower ones. Pan-stick on the lips (no gloss back then) and a generous spraying of Estee Lauder's Youth Dew. A heavy and sultry perfume more suited to the more mature woman but of course that's what you aspired to be at sixteen. At 'fifty something' the situation is reversed. I'm desperately trying to cover up the more mature woman and trying to look ten years younger.

With the help of good face creams, some Botox, a bit of filler, hair extensions, and false eyelashes (all

Sex and the Signposts
Gaynor Evans

the years of wearing them had been a great help) I almost get away with it. The only thing that lets me down is my jaw line, always a dead give-away and the neck of course. But I pile on the creams and wish I had the money for a more permanent fix. Well something seems to be working because I am not short of offers. But the turkey neck may need some attention at some point or I will only attract Roosters!

I was a bit surprised though, when on the previous Friday, I seemed to be attracting a lot of attention from a nice looking young man with huge blue eyes, who seemed intent on chatting me up. The reason for my surprise was that we were in 'The George' a very large and bright pub that serves the cheapest drinks and is always full to bursting with teenagers. I love it though, loud music and lots of energy! But the lighting is not very forgiving. My daughter and her friends are all very attractive and of course younger than me. But, nevertheless, it was me he wanted, it would seem.

This would be the third Friday I had been in his line of fire. It was a warm September evening, I hadn't seen Anthony for some weeks and my holiday in Banus seemed a long way off and frankly I was feeling rampant. The 'getting ready' wine and the couple of gin and tonics had added to my rising libido and he was beginning to look very good to me. He wanted to know where we were going later, I gave him our itinerary and we exchanged numbers

Sex and the Signposts
Gaynor Evans

and he asked if we could catch up later. I said probably. I wasn't sure though, it depended on the other girls and where they wanted to go. We went from bar to bar exchanging banter and having fun, ending up in the bar by the station, the one with the good for my age lighting. He was there hovering with his friends. As I passed, he pulled me towards him and whispered "Can we get out of here?" I pulled back and looked into those big blues eyes and thought, "Mmmm, yes please". I leant in for a kiss, just to see how it felt, and as I thought, it worked. With my temperature rising, I was now keen to play.

My son had told me that he wouldn't be home as he was going to a party and would stay out at a friend's. So a rare opportunity presented itself. My friends had all disappeared outside for a smoke. The smoking ban meant that there was almost the same amount of people outside the bar as in it. As I went to find them, I bumped into another of my previous conquests. We had a bit of a catch up and it was obvious from our body language that we had some history. Blue Eyes had followed me out and was watching me intensely. Laughing and joking, I called to my friends for a bit of diversion. 'Blue eyes' stood guard as I held court between my friends and the other guy. He wasn't going to let me slip off it, would seem.

Well this was fun; and I was revelling in the attention; Eeny meeny miny moe! With which one

Sex and the Signposts
Gaynor Evans

should I go? Deciding that Blue Eyes deserved a chance after his persistent and consistent attention, I smiled sweetly at the guy in front of me, kissed him on the cheek and said bye! Moving across to my friends I explained I was off and then leading 'Blue eyes' by the hand, we grabbed a cab and went home. He gallantly paid the driver and in we went. I switched all the lights on as we went through to the kitchen and pouring us each a drink we settled on the sofa. I was making conversation and he was trying to make out. The large glass of wine in my hand had tipped me over into complete inebriation and he went from looking just 'good' into being Brad Pitt's twin brother. My voice died away as he covered my mouth with his and tried to gain access to my breasts covering the exposed bits in soft kisses. Feeling rather exposed in the bright light of the dining room, and being so unused to 'entertaining' at home, I decided that we should go up to my bedroom where I would feel safer.

This would be a first, in this house and only the second in my bed. My determination to keep my son out of the loop with regards to my liaisons was always paramount in my mind. I did find it rather irritating though, that when he went to visit his father, it was all fine and dandy that Daddy and 'her next door' shared a bed and never an eyebrow was raised. I suppose if I was to give in gracefully and do what all my friends kept suggesting and find a nice steady 'older' man, then that **would** be acceptable. Frankly the idea just didn't appeal,

Sex and the Signposts
Gaynor Evans

maybe it would at some point, but till then the extraordinary lengths I had to go to have a sex life requires forward planning and the good grace of friends and family. As usual, my ex-husband had it easy.

Once in the bedroom, with the door firmly shut, I relaxed a little and the chemistry took over. Frantically pulling at each other's clothes, and kissing in between, we were soon naked. I had the good sense to leave the light off, but there was a small amount of light trickling through the blinds from the street lamps outside. Nevertheless, I couldn't make him out very well so I just had to feel my way. He was very stocky but not that tall, probably about 5ft 10ins. I could feel that he was quite muscular, as I swept my hands over his shoulders and down his back. Kissing still, we sort of fell on the bed in a heap and he quickly took the advantage to roll on top of me. He was grabbing my breasts and running his hands down my body, until he found his target. He quickly slipped his fingers inside me and driven on by my moaning he drove deeper and deeper. I was so aroused now his fingers having driven me to the point of no return. Deciding I should return the favour, and being swept along with drunken passion, I lowered my hand and began grabbing in the dark, wondering what I would find. The moment of truth had arrived! It didn't matter that much as desire had taken over and I would be happy with whatever was on offer. I managed to find it at first grab.

Sex and the Signposts
Gaynor Evans

I could see him watching me, just about, in the dim light, big blue eyes fixed on mine as he drew back in order to help me and gauge my reaction. I took it in my hand, giving it playful strokes and looking up at him I smiled broadly. It was, without doubt the biggest I had ever had the pleasure of looking forward to. It must be at least nine inches, maybe even ten and it was broad. Deciding that I wanted a closer look I sat up and pushed him down and then kneeling between his legs I held it in one hand and began licking it from bottom to top admiring it as I did so. It was simply magnificent! Perfectly straight, no deviations, no bends or wobbles, I was in awe.

Sucking it, in between licks as best I could, it wasn't long before he took control and I was soon on my back again. He took hold of it and with me guiding him he pushed slowly and gently in to me. I was beside myself with excitement and to my surprise, it slid in easily and it felt so good and I was full to bursting. He was masterful and controlled and knew exactly how to use it. I was swept away in a complete frenzy of sexual enjoyment and had completely abandoned myself to this experience. He had been very drunk and I was surprised that it hadn't affected him in anyway, and said as much. His reply was "Don't you worry about that; you are going to be up all night". My reply was a smile and some more kissing and the frenzy continued.

Sex and the Signposts
Gaynor Evans

My bed was making the most awful squeaking noises and so was I, when I was brought back from cloud nine inches by a loud bang! "What was that noise?" I said, stopping him. I had heard the noise before, but in my drunken state, I couldn't place it. Then the fog cleared and I leapt off the bed. Oh no! It was the front door, meaning my son was home! Grabbing my dressing gown, I leant over the bed and whispering to him to be quiet and not to move, I made for the door. None of the doors in my two bedroom terrace shut properly, with the exception of the bathroom. I had no lock on the bedroom one and as usual it had sprung open once the front door had been slammed.

It wouldn't be unusual for my son to come into my room to let me know he was home and have a chat. Heart pounding, I ran for the stairs, only to find him at the top of them. "Hi luv" I said, as calmly as possible, "I thought you weren't coming home?" "Well," he said "I decided I wanted to sleep in my own bed, and I'm a bit drunk and feel sick!" "Well, I wish you had phoned me" I said, "It's a bit awkward, I have someone here." His glare, (reminiscent of his father the day he left when I asked if he had everything) was followed by gritted teeth. "Who is it and how old is he?" I replied "No one you know, and he'll be leaving in a minute, just go to bed and I will show him out." He started to protest, but I ushered him into his room, which is right next to mine by the way, and said "Just get to bed." Sulking, like a giant two year old, he shut the

Sex and the Signposts
Gaynor Evans

door in my face.

Going back into my room, I crept over to the bed and slid back in saying, to my well endowed friend that we would have to be quiet and wait for my son to fall asleep. The only good thing was that he was likely to do that quickly as he was drunk. I couldn't risk him popping out of his room just as I was showing Blue Eyes to the door. Blue Eyes himself was in a bit of a panic and asked me how old my son was and how big was he? I suppose the 6ft 4ins can be a bit intimidating!

We lay side by side like planks of wood not daring to stir and I was thinking typical! The one time I take a chance, and I get caught in the throes. Ten minutes passed and all was quiet, and I curled into my lover, who was now struggling to stay awake, and suddenly we were kissing again. I was now feeling very frustrated and rather irritable as our lovemaking hadn't reached its conclusion and what there had been was so yummy that frankly I wanted more. We quietly resumed, but stopped almost straight away as the bed sounded like it needed oiling. Damn it! Thinking on my feet (well my back actually) I threw the duvet cover on the floor over by the window and as far away from my son's adjoining wall as possible and then placed the chair up against the door. We got on the duvet and tried again. There wasn't much room and my head kept sliding under the dressing table. We managed for a while, but it was just too difficult and to be honest,

Sex and the Signposts
Gaynor Evans

enjoying sex quietly is not one of my best subjects. Getting to my feet and pulling him up, I whispered that we'd better go down stairs. As we passed my son's room, I sent Blue Eyes down the stairs and I peeped in. My son was sound asleep.

We went into the lounge and flopping on the sofa, we tried again. It was ok, but the mood was broken and I was just too anxious to really get into it. The thought of my son and this other young man coming face to face was too horrible to contemplate. Blue Eyes and I said our goodbyes and off he went.

My son and I discussed the matter in the cold light of our hangovers. He wasn't a happy chappy, but as I explained I wouldn't normally have dared to bring someone home. I reasoned that it was **him** that had changed his plans, and if he had come home in the morning as arranged, he would have been none the wiser. I, for my part, would have made sure that 'Blue Eyes' was long gone. We agreed that it was just one of those things and maybe a phone call next time would help. Our close relationship was not affected and continued as before. Sometimes though, I found myself wistfully wishing that I had been up all night with my 'Cloud Nine Inches'. He certainly had hidden assets, oh! and as it turns out, a girlfriend. Typical!!

"A hard man is good to find"
Mae West

Sex and the Signposts
Gaynor Evans

Chapter Five
RADIOACTIVE ROMANCE

After my first couple of toyboy encounters, I was both encouraged and intrigued. If I could arouse this amount of interest in person, I wonder what I could do on the internet. One Sunday morning, some months before whilst looking at my pine tree and reading the newspaper - The Mail, I had been leafing through the magazine supplement, when I came across an article on a new website for the 'older woman seeking the younger man'! Toyboywarehouse.com sounded fun and I got out my diary and scribbled the web address in the back. When I get out of this prison, I thought, I will give that a try.

It was some time later in the office when I joked with Chloe that I remember something about this website for toyboys. It was lunchtime so she quickly googled it and came up with it in an instant. "Go on" she pleaded "put up a profile". I hesitated, I was already on Facebook which she had entreated me to do and this had proved quite entertaining. Then I said "Oh what the hell, go on". Five minutes later, I was on the site; picture loaded and called 'Gbird'.

I didn't really pay much attention for the first few weeks but used to log on to see if I had any interest. To my surprise I did - loads of it! Lots of cards telling me "you're gorgeous", "you float my boat"

Sex and the Signposts
Gaynor Evans

or winks. It was very ego boosting even if some of the guys were less than appetising. Some months later, when having moved and got settled in my Victorian terrace with views of the Co-operative, I got bored one evening. My daughter had got me a reconditioned laptop on the cheap (I'm still using it now). Winter had set in and I was cosy and warm in my front room, glass of wine in one hand and was updating my Facebook page, when I decided to take another look at TBW (as it is known in all the best circles). It required me to upgrade to silver membership if I was to read or send any messages. It was only a tenner for a month and I thought 'in for a penny in for a pound'. I had a number of messages, looked at them all and the pictures of the senders and decided to reply to some of them.

This was uncharted waters and I had no idea how to respond or what was expected, but I tried a few things and started dialoguing with various 'toyboys'. They were all very complimentary and spoke in terms of "wish I was there with you hun" or "you're so hot you're making me horny". Some couldn't wait to talk very explicitly about their desires and offered to send me more daring photos. This would be the start of my collection of 'Willy Pictures', (I had kept the one that my Ascot Stallion had sent me). Once my phone number had been handed over a few texts would be followed by the inevitable picture of the sender's privates in various stages of arousal.

Sex and the Signposts
Gaynor Evans

At first I was shocked and then I found it funny and would roar with laughter at the various shapes, sizes and types that would appear, as if by magic! They became of great interest to my friends who would grab my phone to see the latest arrival. One night after a lively evening out with the girlfriends I received a text from a gorgeous hunk with muscles to die for that had been sending me messages for a while. Without asking permission he sent me 'the picture'. It was quite clear, but for some reason, probably bad lighting, the erection he was so proud of was bright green and had an eerie glow! Laughing out loud I speculated as to whether it was radioactive? Perhaps that's what happens to willies when they are sent via mobile phone! With tears rolling down my face, I sent something appropriate back and saving the picture for future amusement, I went to bed.

My collection of willy pictures was infamous locally, and it amazed me that these guys didn't mind exposing themselves so publicly. I was often asked to send a picture back and used to find a nice fully clothed one and wing it off to them. I knew that wasn't what they wanted, but if they thought I was going to send a picture of my private parts to their phone they were very much mistaken. You never know where it would end up and they might even show it to their friends! It got to the point where I had so many different ones on my phone I was seriously thinking of setting up my own website called 'Willy's are us', headed up of course

Sex and the Signposts
Gaynor Evans

by 'Mr Green'. It certainly would have added to the argument that all men are equal but some are definitely more equal than others. Over the course of months, I deleted most of them keeping just a few and one in particular that could only be described as magnificent. This man could have made a fortune in the Porn industry.

My first actual internet date was a disaster. The young man concerned, highly intelligent obviously, but with no dress sense, nothing like his picture and with an unexpected stutter! I wondered why he had never taken up my invitation for a chat on the phone! It was really bad. We had met for a drink and it was a very painful hour and a half. I had instructed my daughter to ring me mid-date to check on my safety. I wasn't in any danger, unless being assaulted by spit counted. I felt really sorry for him and was polite and friendly and had to fight to stop myself finishing his sentences. Making my excuses, I left as early as possible. But not before he had lunged at me for the inevitable goodnight kiss. Not knowing the right way to extricate myself, it ended in a full blown snog. He certainly didn't suffer with delayed lips and I sort of made all the right noises and then made my escape.

Unfortunately, he was smitten and had already text me by the time I got home. This was followed by three emails and another couple of texts (for obvious reasons he didn't try to ring me!). Feeling dreadful about it, I tried to find the right words to put him off. It wasn't easy, I realised that he was already struggling with lack of confidence and probably had little experience with women. I suppose he was hoping an older woman might treat him more kindly and give him a chance. I didn't want to hurt his feelings anymore than I had to, but I already had other prospective dates in the loop and there just wasn't any point dragging it out. So I sent him this:

"Hi Richard thanks for the emails. Sorry for late reply I have been incredibly busy. It was nice meeting you the other night, but I have been seeing others from the website and on reflection I just don't feel that there was enough chemistry between us. Sorry! And good luck."

I pressed send and breathed a sigh of relief. Not unexpectedly, I didn't get a reply but he did email me some months later. I decided to ignore it.

This experience could have put me off internet dating all together but I reasoned that the only way was up. I had been receiving emails via TBW from a young Australian. He seemed intelligent and I liked the look of him too. He was tall with a strong chiselled face and a nice smile. He was working in London and had gone home for the Christmas holidays. He suggested meeting up when he returned in January and I agreed, straight back on the horse I thought. His emails were quite funny and amusing and with just a hint of sexual

Sex and the Signposts
Gaynor Evans

innuendo. He sent me a few pictures of himself and I reciprocated.

He was very complimentary and said he would like to 'pamper' me. Not sure what that meant but figured it might have sex in it somewhere. As he promised, on his return, he sent me an email and we set a date for the following Monday. This he cancelled by email on Monday morning. He had caught the flu and was very poorly, could we reschedule for next week. I made sympathetic noises and said yes of course, but I was disappointed and had been really looking forward to meeting him. Cancelled dates are the curse of the internet; I was to find out later.

The week came and went and it was Monday again and this time he was definitely coming. He travelled to meet me by train early in the evening. It was quite a trek for him as he lived on the other side of London, but he made light of it. I liked him immediately; he had plenty to say and I loved the 'Aussie drawl' and gratefully he looked like his pictures. We got on like a house on fire and he was certainly making me 'hot'. We spent a couple of hours together. He was respectful, courteous and I was getting a little excited about the end of the evening and the inevitable kiss. He actually asked if it was ok to kiss me, I nodded in agreement, let the kissing commence. Wow! It took my breath away and I could feel my excitement rising in all the right areas. He got a little over-excited too but when I drew back to get control of myself, he immediately followed my lead and did the same.

That gesture was to convince me that I was in control and this made him more endearing and I decided there and then that I wanted to have him. And so have him I did! He came back a few weeks later and we spent a lovely afternoon together exploring each other's bodies (more details to follow). This was to be the start of my Aussie obsession, which was to span many months and was almost my undoing!

Sex and the Signposts
Gaynor Evans

Chapter Six
BRAINS, BRAWN AND BOURGUIGNON

My first Valentine's Day as a singleton was looming up fast. The previous year, although technically still married, a few girls and I had gathered for an Anti-Valentine party. We opened champagne and spent the evening pulling to pieces the men (or not) in our lives. We were all without a date as such and the amount of pressure to have one is quite shocking.

All your happily married friends and loved-up acquaintances are waxing lyrical about where they are going for the intimate dinner and how big the bouquet of flowers was that arrived by special delivery and what the card said. Frankly it can be quite disheartening if you don't have a man or even worse your living with someone that doesn't harbour one romantic thought about you anymore.

My ex-husband had always been very romantic and was BIG on Valentine's Day which made the lack of attention even more painful. He used to send me roses, usually delivered to my office, and we would go out for a romantic dinner and then come home and make love. Ah those were the days!. His cards were always the kind stating his undying love - always. Well he had definitely changed his mind about that!

Sex and the Signposts
Gaynor Evans

This year I knew I was going to feel the void quite acutely. When my daughters lived at home and were both sporting boyfriends our house used to look and smell like a florist shop and I loved it, flower arranging being one of my favourite things to do.

So Valentine's Day 2009 became something of a mission. I was determined, by hook or by crook, that I would not spend it alone and decided that some sort of date was required to keep my morale up! The whole thing was made worse by the fact that St Valentine has decided to fire his bow and arrow on a Saturday, the traditional date night of the week. No pressure then?

I had been chatting on line via my new found friend - toyboywarehouse.com, to a number of seemingly nice young men but didn't, as yet, have any offers. Reflecting on this it occurred to me that a toyboy probably wouldn't want to spend such a 'Big' occasion with an older woman, in case it was misconstrued. I had also added something to my Facebook page called 'Are you interested?' and was receiving loads of messages from a variety of men all ages and types. Some of the pictures that popped up made me laugh out loud but one or two seemed quite interesting so I began replying.

One of these guys 'Mike' seemed nice and was probably about forty, so quite a respectable age. My laptop and I were rarely apart these days and

Sex and the Signposts
Gaynor Evans

most evenings I would be sat in my cosy front room, multitasking, between the laptop, the TV, and a glass of wine.

The chatting on-line was time consuming but also quite intoxicating as the men involved threw the words Hun, Babe and gorgeous in my direction. This was such a nice change from the ones I had been hearing as my marriage gasped for breath. In the last two years there had been no soft words or confidence boosting compliments. Just bitter, angry arguments and insults, yes lots of insults, coming from its dying throat. So to be called hun or babe and to be told you look sexy and hot, gave my ego a much needed stroke and just made me feel better.

You have to be careful that when the love has died in a marriage you don't believe your own bad press. It's hard to come out unscathed and not riddled with doubt and self-loathing. The partner trying to wriggle out of his commitments conscience free, will do all he can to make it **your fault** in every which way he can. You need to be thick skinned and have been a defence lawyer in a previous life.

My Ex would often pick a fight just to back up his own somewhat rocky self-esteem and reassure himself that he was completely justified in his behaviour. Of course me, in blissful ignorance would often take his slatings to heart, until of course I found out the truth. After that I gave as good as I got and even had him questioning whether or not he

Sex and the Signposts
Gaynor Evans

wanted to actually leave me. Of course I was just playing with him, cat to mouse, the writing was not only on the wall it was tattooed!!!

So Mike and I continued our online 'wooing' and I found out he was from the East of England, about a three and a half hours drive from me. I almost gave up at this point thinking that it was just too far and the chances of us ever meeting up were very remote. At some point, we progressed to texting and finally a couple of phone calls. We got on well and I found out that he had a fair bit of banter even if he did have a 'country bumpkin' accent. I found it quite sweet.

During one lengthy phone call I drop into the conversation the subject of Valentine's Day and he says sadly that he does not have a date. I had been partaking of a couple of glasses of wine and at this point, and feeling brave, I suggest that I cook him dinner. He is quick in responding with the words "great idea". He doesn't seem to have any problem with the distance as he drives around a lot and he will bring the champagne. It's not lost on me that if he drives to me and then helps me drink the champagne then driving home won't be an option. Thinking about this I reason with myself that the sofa was always available. Having made a firm arrangement with him I am quite pleased with myself, the panic was over, I had achieved my goal; I had a date for St Valentines Night! My son was

Sex and the Signposts
Gaynor Evans

going to visit a friend for an overnight stay, so I was sorted! Marvellous!

I must have checked out Mike's profile page on Facebook a hundred times over the next few days. He seemed a safe bet, a family man, divorced, into football, not bad looking and a respectable age, my dalliances with toyboys were getting notoriously younger so at least this man was in his forth decade.

I cast my thoughts in the direction of what to put on the menu, but that was easy. My usual first dinner date offering was always the same 'Beef Bourguignon' served with rice and salad followed by homemade 'Chocolate brandy mousse'. These were two dishes that could be prepared in advance and leave you calm and in control and able to sit at the table making small talk and being charming. Plus there is nothing better than the smell of the beef and wine cooking in the oven; it wafts around the house adding atmosphere and ambiance. It also has a brilliant effect on the appetite; by the time you get to the table you are ravenous.

So the week passed without event and Kate and I decided to go out on Friday as she didn't have a date on Saturday and was in need of a lively night. We went to all our usual bars and pubs. Moving from bar to bar and chatting to familiar faces, we eventually ended up at our final destination (the bar by the station with the good for my age lighting!). Standing at the bar as we ordered our drinks we

Sex and the Signposts
Gaynor Evans

spotted two guys we knew quite well. In fact one of them I knew very well, intimately in fact. His name was Kevin and I had met him by association, he was friends with various members of the family and was strictly out of bounds. He was in his late twenties and a nice guy.

He was about 6ft tall and had strikingly dark eyes and strawberry blonde hair, but his main attraction was his body. He spent a lot of time in the gym and it showed in all the right places. He had big biceps, a weakness of mine, and a honed and toned six pack and big shoulders. He was quite a hunk. I had met him at a family party the year before and had gone over to admire the biceps, giving them a little squeeze. We had a little chat and this turned into outrageous flirting and at one point he lunged at me for a kiss and his friend had to drag him off. Just as well, I thought, family present and all that, plus I was still technically in my marriage. It turned out that I had known his father many years before and we had a lot of mutual acquaintances. So as I said 'strictly out of bounds'.

It was much later and during my just post marriage phase that we kept bumping into each other. The flirting continued in earnest and he was all over me like a rash and I began to feel quite excited by his attention. He was always quite blatant and used to tell me he got a 'hard on' as soon as I came into view. This for me, who had been sidelined, after twenty years of marriage for a younger woman, was

Sex and the Signposts
Gaynor Evans

hugely flattering. We exchanged numbers at some point and we would text each other here and there.

For safety I had him stored in my phone as 'Muscleman' and I was called 'Emma' in his. He made it quite clear that he wanted to take me to bed and very tempted as I was I just didn't want to upset anyone. But we were both single, as he had broken up with a long term girlfriend some months before. I deliberated over it for a long time and one night at a party I even had to sneak off alone, because he was systematically attacking all my defences and I was weakening.

In the end, when the opportunity presented itself some months later, I just couldn't resist. The pull of those muscles was just too strong. One evening he had an empty house and we arranged a covert and secret rendezvous by text. I left my friends at the wine bar and said I was going home and he collected me in a dark car park. He lived a few miles away and as we pulled up outside his house I was aware that my stomach was churning and I was feeling really quite nervous. He took me by the hand and led me in. I liked the hand holding; it was caring and protective and went a little way to reassuring me. Once inside, with the door firmly shut, he began an assault on my body that I can only describe as being ravaged.

After the months of anticipation and unfulfilled desire, it felt heavenly. Taking his shirt over his

Sex and the Signposts
Gaynor Evans

head he revealed his gorgeous torso and I ran my hands over his arms and stomach and gasping with delight and god, was he fit! Kissing him from the shoulders down, I ran my tongue over his rippling six-pack. This sent him into frenzy and overwhelmed by his months of pent up desire, he manhandled me up the stairs and into his bedroom. Once inside and still being joined at the lips we managed to get the rest of our clothes off. We leapt on the bed and lying side by side he ran his hands up my thighs and slipped his fingers in, as if my body was familiar territory. "Christ" he whispered "you are so wet."

Frankly the sight of his naked body was enough to make a nun give up the vows. I was so aroused by now that I was impatient to have him and he could not contain his delight at finally getting me into bed. He offered his fingers to my mouth by way of demonstration, and I licked them sensuously. He then spent ages working magic with his tongue and when the moment came I was more than ready. Poising himself on his strong arms above me, he found his way inside with ease. He commanded so much power behind every thrust; I was delirious with passion and responded by moaning loudly and grabbing his gorgeous buttocks, forcing him further in. After what seemed like forever, with my head pounding on the headboard, we were spent and curling up together he put his arm protectively around me.

Sex and the Signposts
Gaynor Evans

It was the first time I had slept with another man in the same bed, so this was quite a milestone. I felt like I had finally 'arrived'. In the morning more strong, powerful and overwhelming sex followed and by the time he dropped me home I was ready to go back to bed for some sleep. It had been quite an adventure and I felt that having spent the night in another man's house I had really moved on.

We managed to keep our liaisons secret and met up a few more times after that. But as it was always very cloak and dagger, the opportunities didn't crop up very often. It had been quite a long time since our last meeting and yet here he was before me, wearing a tight t-shirt that showed every muscle off to its best advantage. We kissed hello and I gave the biceps a familiar squeeze. He whispered to me that as usual I had made his trousers tighter. I giggled and said shame because the chances of us being able to slip off anywhere were remote. My son being firmly ensconced at home and his house mates were there with him and came into the 'must never know' category.

He touched me at every opportunity, a stroke here and a grope there. He was obviously full of testosterone and I could sense that he wanted to rip my clothes off. Frankly he would have met with little resistance; I was keen to give those muscles another close inspection. Damn it! This was one of those times when I wished I lived alone.

Sex and the Signposts
Gaynor Evans

Sexually frustrated I went home and woke up the following morning still with him on my mind. I had lots to do with my Valentine's dinner to organise and the house to clean. But feeling the need, I sent him a text saying "Emma woke up with muscles on her mind". He answered immediately "Kevin went to bed alone and frustrated". Texts flew back and forth, both of us translating our physical frustrations into written dialogue

Kevin
'I wanted u so much last night'

Emma
'Me 2 Hun u were looking hot'

Kevin
'So frustrating the last couple of times we met we Haven't been able to do anything!'

Emma
'I know it is frustrating, I do have an empty house coming up soon'

Kevin
'Don't know what it is about u but u turn me on so much! Yeah? Cool let me kno wen should be able to make sum nights'

Emma
'Ok sexy I will'

Sex and the Signposts
Gaynor Evans

Kevin
'shame it's not now tho you really should take advantage of me in this mood'

Emma
'Believe me I want to hun. Yum!'

Checking the time at this point I realised it was already 1.30pm in the afternoon and my date was due at 7.30pm. So I had about seven hours to get all my housework done, prepare the food and make myself look gorgeous. Reluctantly putting my phone down I go into the kitchen and putting some music on I get stuck in. I started chopping and slicing but could not get Kevin's muscles out of my head and got very excited about one huge carrot that reminded me of something else. Taking my frustration out on it, I chopped it firmly into little pieces.

My son ambled into the kitchen foraging for food. "Mum make me breakfast" hardly breakfast, I thought, more like lunch! I rustled up a bacon sarnie, his staple diet at the weekend, and we chatted about what he was doing for the evening and with his mobile stuck firmly to his ear in one hand and the sandwich in the other he slumped in front of the TV. His phone was going off constantly and coming back into kitchen with his plate he said he would be going to James's a bit earlier as they wanted to go somewhere. "Ok luv" I

Sex and the Signposts
Gaynor Evans

answered and "what time would that be?" "Dunno" he grunted "bout four".

Dinner prepared and in the oven, cooking slowly, chocolate mousse made with double the amount of brandy added (I might need the extra shot later depending on how my date goes) chilling in the fridge. I whisked about dusting, hoovering and cleaning. I went upstairs to tidy my bedroom and wondered whether my date was going to ever get this far. Straightening the sheets and pondering whether they would need changing in the morning, a light suddenly went on in my head! Jack was leaving at 4pm and my date was due at 7.30pm. Here was a three hour window of opportunity. An empty house, I wonder if? No, I couldn't, could I? I mean it wouldn't be right would it? Seeing two men in one day?

Not that I had any intention of sleeping with my dinner date, but it was a possibility. He was of course an unknown quantity, whereas Kevin was tried, tested and definitely approved! No! Best not complicate things, pushing the thought of the six-pack firmly away, I ran a bath and set about the beautifying process.

Getting out of the bath and wrapped in a towel I plonked myself on the bed. It was now about 4pm. I lay back on the cushions staring at the ceiling. The six-pack homed into view followed by the biceps and the dark brown eyes and, oh sod it! I

Sex and the Signposts
Gaynor Evans

was fed up with wrestling with my conscience and decided that I would rather be wrestling with Kevin instead. Reaching over, I picked up my phone and sent him a text. "wot are u doing this afternoon?" The immediate reply was "I'm out shopping and then going to the gym why?" I explained about the empty house and then added that I had to be out by seven, followed by a large question mark. "Really" he replied "let me see wot I can do" followed by a smiley face. I carried on getting ready for my 'other date' and began pacing around like a caged animal.

A little later Jack called up the stairs "bye mum, I'm off". Good the coast was clear. He knew I had a date that night so wouldn't be back. I picked up my phone. Still nothing and the suspense was killing me. I decided to get ready, just in case. I opened up my make-up bag and started looking through my wardrobe to find something to wear, black dress I think, oh and the boots, everyone loves the boots. I was rummaging through my underwear draw when I heard my phone chirp. About time "I could be there by about 6.15 is that any good?" God that would be cutting it fine, but by now all sense of reason had gone out of the window along, it would seem, with my morality! "Ok, but earlier if u can" I replied. I then text my evening date and told him to come a little later as "something had come up" well that was the general idea anyway I thought to myself giggling. I am very badly behaved! Kevin had said he would let me know when he was on his

Sex and the Signposts
Gaynor Evans

way and not to bother to get dressed as we wouldn't have much time. Thinking 'cheeky devil' I proceeded to cover myself in body lotion from head to toe.

By 5.30pm I was all ready, dinner was cooking nicely, I had all my make-up on and my hair was done. I was wearing just some nice underwear (no not 'winter flock' by La Senza!) under my silky dressing gown. I waited anxiously, clutching my mobile in one hand, and my glass of 'getting ready wine', in the other. Suddenly my phone went off the message read "Get your clothes off I'm coming round!" Ten minutes later I opened the door to my 'muscleman' Grinning broadly at me he greeted me with the words "Happy Valentine's day" and before I could reply, he picked me up and kissing me hard he pinned me up against the wall.

A frenzy of kissing and fondling followed before we raced up the stairs hand in hand and into my bedroom. Enjoying his muscles once more as he poised himself above me, he took me with power, passion and speed. We lay for a short while together panting and catching our breath. I was aware that the clock was ticking and he, thinking I had to be out by seven was happy to go having got rid of his pent up frustrations. I lead him to the door and laughing like a couple of naughty children we said our goodbyes. Grabbing a towel I went back into the bathroom for a shower and to get ready for round two.

Sex and the Signposts
Gaynor Evans

My date arrived on time and bearing not one but two bottles of Champagne, definitely scoring some early brownie points. He was a lovely guy who seemed quite intelligent and we had a nice evening eating, drinking and talking. My Beef Bourguignon was a great success and I managed to keep a straight face when he asked me what it was that had "Come up?" I lied beautifully.

When we retired to the lounge and got cosy on the sofa and the kissing started it was pleasant but not 'up there'. I distracted him by putting on DVDs. I went to bed alone for obvious reasons, although I did keep expecting to hear his footsteps on the stairs and therefore didn't sleep very well. I think my date took the fact that he was lodged on the sofa quite well, although he probably moaned about it in private, having travelled a long way.

But we did have a nice evening and he was well fed. I don't think I would have done anything differently even if my 'knight in shining muscles' hadn't swooped in and stolen the advantage. It had been a memorable St. Valentine's Day in more ways than one, even if I had been a little greedy. My punishment for such gluttony was that I never did get up close and personal with those muscles again although you never know when opportunity will knock! As for my dinner companion, we spoke once or twice but I just wasn't feeling it! Oh well,

Sex and the Signposts
Gaynor Evans

such is life and lucky for me the sexy Australian was still in the loop.

Sex and the Signposts
Gaynor Evans

Chapter Seven
WALTZING MATILDA

The day had started badly, management meeting in branch at 9am so focus, focus, focus! Besides being preoccupied with whether the Aussie toyboy would turn up for our date that evening, I was somewhat concerned about Matilda, my baby granddaughter. My daughter and the baby were staying with me, due to the demise of her relationship, not an easy arrangement. I only had a 'two up two down' Victorian terrace now, since the four bedrooms, two bathrooms, with tree views, had been sold. My son, of course, had opted to stay in London with me, and not go to 'Rose Cottage' in the Norfolk countryside with his Dad, so now baby made four. I had given my daughter and the baby my bedroom, so I either slept on the sofa or went to my other daughter's flat to sleep. My car could be seen whipping backwards and forwards late evenings and early mornings and my life was rather over-full! Returning that morning, I came in and picked up my gorgeous granddaughter to give her a kiss when I noticed that one of her lips seemed a little blue. Matilda was otherwise on good form but she had been a bit chesty. I told my daughter to keep a close eye on her and I would check in later.

The meeting was tough, the recession was biting hard and we were trying to find a strategy to cope in the now, very precarious, world of recruitment. We broke for lunch at about twelve and I checked my phone, still no messages from my toyboy with excuses of "so sorry can't make it tonight" in fact no messages at all, not even the sort I am used to receiving from him, going into great detail of what he'd like to do to me, when and if he gets here.

I decided to go get lunch and in the process check in on the baby. My house is just across the road from the office, so I called in. I didn't like what I saw. The blue patch on her lip was still there and to my mind she seemed a little 'bluish' around the cheeks as well. Without further ado, I gave my daughter Laura instructions to take her to the Casualty department at the hospital, just to be on the safe side. (Thoughts of heart conditions or chest infections came to mind and although she seemed fine, better to be safe than sorry.)

Returning to the office, I decided to text my toyboy for affirmation of our date. "Hi just checking that u still on track 4 later?" I pressed the send button before I had a chance to change my mind - no news is good news - but I just wanted to make sure. Five minutes passed no reply. Then ten minutes, still no reply. Eventually, after checking my phone a million times with that sinking feeling that I was about to be told that "something had come up". He finally responded with "yes indeed - was I?" Was I? I'd been on the track and five times round it already. It had only taken him two months to get to see me this time. However, that aside, I was quietly excited by the prospect of seeing him again, and

Sex and the Signposts
Gaynor Evans

what would follow. In the back of my mind was the nagging worry of 'hope the baby is ok'.

Back to work, focus, focus. My daughter rang at 3.00pm. She had been seen by the Doctor and they said that all the signs were normal, oxygen levels etc, but as a precaution they just wanted to call the Paediatric Registrar. So she was waiting. Reassured, I took my maternal head off and put my work head back on.

The afternoon went quickly. I had a number of things to do before I could relax into the anticipation of the evening. I had to go home and feed the dogs, as my daughter couldn't. Rushing in, I met my son eighteen going on fifteen, 6ft 4ins with the appetite of an elephant and apparently in need of a shirt for work. "Have you seen one mum?" he asked. "Yes" I said "it's on the line, drying, but it will need ironing." A look of bewilderment covers his face; he is not familiar with the word 'ironing' and even less familiar with the activity. "Ok" I said "I will get it in" but no time for ironing, I would throw it in the tumble drier! I kicked off my stilettos, so that I could rush about without breaking a leg and hurried into the garden, nearly tripping over the dogs as I did so, barefoot and paying no attention, I tread straight into a pile of fresh dog poo! Lovely! Hot date in less than an hour and now I'll have to go and shower my feet and between my toes - Yuk!

Sex and the Signposts
Gaynor Evans

Hopping back into the house and wiping the worst off, I go to the bathroom and shower and thoroughly wash my feet. So, son's shirt in tumble drier, dogs fed, wine and beer collected, back into the car and down to my other daughter's flat that she was kindly letting me use for my assignation. (Due to my daughter and baby's return this flat is now my refuge and second home.) Putting the beer in the fridge I checked out 'my' bedroom as I now refer to it. Removing Harvey, the giant furry rabbit, from the pillow where he sits, a present from her Nan, very sweet but not quite the right thing to have staring at you when you are getting naked with a young man. I look for somewhere to put him. The room is not very big and stacked up against the wall is a pile of over full suitcases that belong to my other daughter; we are all housing bits of her previous life. Oh well, no time to set the scene, it would just have to do! Plonking Harvey down on top of the suitcases, I rushed out of the flat and back into the car. On to the stables to get the horse in from the fields and fed, the clock was ticking….

My phone went off. My toyboy was on schedule and should arrive at the station by 6.00pm. It was already 5.45pm - better get a move on, just time for a quick freshen up. Then my phone starts ringing; this time it's my daughter, good hopefully she's home. But no! The Consultant has decided that as a precaution they wanted to take some blood tests from the baby and want to admit her and my daughter overnight. Great! Mother-head back on

Sex and the Signposts
Gaynor Evans

"was she gonna be ok till I could get there?" "Yes" friend with her so not to worry, carry on regardless.

By now the train was on its way. I had no choice but to carry on, but feeling like the worst mother in the world, I called my other daughter for input. "Don't worry Mum, you go and enjoy yourself. You deserve some 'Me' time and you've been waiting for him to come over for so long…Laura and the baby will be fine. She's in the best place and her friends there." I felt a bit better and I immediately took 'Mother' head off and put the 'seductive older lover' head on. My life is never simple!

I manage to get to the station just as the train pulls in. I haven't seen him for some weeks and there he is smiling broadly bounding over to my car looking gorgeous in a suit. He leans in and gives me a big kiss on the lips, lovely, but he does look ridiculous in my pink lipstick. I whisk him off to the flat, roof down, sun shining and wind blowing in my hair. God, I hope he hasn't spotted my extensions. I thought! We park up at the flat and as I put the roof back on the car, I notice that I'd left Matilda's rattle on the back seat. Hope he hadn't spotted it. He fondly refers to me as his "sexy M.I.L.F." I hadn't got around to telling him that I was now elevated to G.I.L.F. status!

We go into the flat, music on, wine opened, a few pleasantries, and lots of kissing. A few more pleasantries and lots of groping and we were under

Sex and the Signposts
Gaynor Evans

starters orders - yummy. I lead him by the hand into the bedroom. I have never seen anyone get a suit off so quickly and there he is naked before me. He pulls my dress over my head and immediately starts to wrestle with my bra pulling it down to expose my nipples sucking on them really hard. We kiss frantically in between manoeuvring ourselves on to the bed.

I kiss his broad shoulders and run my fingers through his chest hair (he has just the right amount). He pushes me back and dives between my legs. I am lying across the bed and he is now kneeling on the floor. He is tall and beds with ends don't lend themselves very easily to his favourite pastime so we have to be inventive. "Ooh I love the ginge" he moans as he dives in tongue first. Hmm, let me explain, although sporting a full head of blond locks I was a redhead in a previous life. As I got older the colour faded to blonde, on my head anyways. The rest of me remained true to my roots so I am still a 'ginger minge'. I often feel the need to explain this bit but the Aussie loves it with a passion and the hairier the better. (My ex-husband used to complain about the amount of hair I sprouted down there and had given me quite a complex, nice then to find someone who can't get enough of it).

My Aussie spends a long time worshiping it taking me to dizzy heights and then standing up he offers his cock up to my mouth for me to return the favour, which I do with relish. Extremely aroused

Sex and the Signposts
Gaynor Evans

now, I am desperate to have him inside me and, whispering that in his ear, he leaps across to the side of the bed where he dropped his trousers and produces a condom.

He is fanatical about using them, which is fine with me. Adept at getting them on in a matter of seconds he is swiftly inside me taking my breath away as he plunges in. He drives in an out of me hard and strong causing me to moan loudly and I have a fleeting thought about my daughter's neighbours and hope they can't hear me. He keeps his bright blue eyes firmly fixed on mine to watch my delight, making things more intense. Feeling the need to be more in control I push him over and climb on top just too slow things down a little. I take him back Inside me and ride him gently, picking up speed until I am totally lost in the moment. Whispering to me softly he says "I want to take you from behind" I get up to oblige as he stands up and I roll over.

A minute passes and I'm still waiting, backside in the air. Then I hear his voice behind me "Erm the bed has moved" "What?" I say, he repeats "the bed has moved". I roll over onto my side to look and to my amazement the bed has gone from one side of the room to the other and is now rammed up against the bloody suitcases. I've heard of the earth moving but the bed?! Poor Harvey had been knocked unceremoniously on to the floor or maybe he was just covering his eyes! My Aussie shaking his head says "Shall I move it back?" Giggling loudly I say

Sex and the Signposts
Gaynor Evans

"Nah" and pull him back down to the bed, kissing him some more before he turns me over to take me from behind.

I am almost exhausted by the time he says "I'm coming" and taking himself out and whipping off the condom, I turn over and he comes all over my breasts. It feels warm and sticky and I love it. Running my fingers through it, I lick my fingers before collapsing on the bed, I put my head on his chest and he holds me while we recover and chatting quietly we laugh about the moving bed. I again cast my thoughts in the direction of my daughter's neighbours. Hope they hadn't heard us; we obviously had been very carried away. (They will think my daughter is having a really good evening if they had.) After ten minutes or so my Aussie suggests we have a cigarette I nod in agreement.

Getting up from the bed I quickly put my underwear on and he starts buttoning up his shirt. "Better throw that condom away" he says and starts to look for it. It's nowhere to be seen. We hunt high and low but there is absolutely no sign of it. I get on my hands and knees to look under the bed and rummage through the bed covers, with no luck. "Don't worry" I say "we can look again in a minute." We go to the kitchen to put the kettle on, lighting cigarettes, and settle back on the sofa chatting happily, both in the afterglow that follows great sex.

Sex and the Signposts
Gaynor Evans

One of the things I like about this man is the fact that he has many sides. He is a professional, suit and tie man, highly educated and can hold a good conversation and is witty and makes me laugh. But he is also a bad boy. He smokes and drinks too much; he's definitely one of the boys and makes it clear he goes on benders. I imagine he has dabbled in drugs and the first time I got him naked I was amazed to see he was sporting a number of exotic tattoos all hidden under the suit. There is a lot of banter between us but he is also complimentary and respectful.

As a package he ticks a lot of boxes. His bright blue eyes flash with intelligence and although he wears glasses they don't detract from his charm. I think Australian Clark Kent although I'm not sure he would look quite as good in the superman leotard as although he has great shoulders the rest of him is quite lean. Anyway all in all, I am quite smitten and I found myself wondering wistfully why they didn't make them like him when I was younger.

Checking his watch, he says he better go. He has a long journey home and quite a few train changes. I pick up my car keys and as we pass the bedroom he stops and says "Oh, what about the condom?" I reply that I will come back and look. (Last thing I want is my very tolerant daughter finding a used condom.) I drop him back at the station kissing him a passionate goodbye and with promises of a return

Sex and the Signposts
Gaynor Evans

visit, he disappears into the building.

I immediately put my mother head back on (I've swopped heads more times than Wurzel Gummidge today) and zoom up the road to the hospital. I find my daughter and granddaughter in a room of their own and all seems well. They are keeping her in just as a precaution and to wait for the blood test results. Her friend, still in the room asks me where I've been as I look dishevelled and am sporting 'sex hair'. I regale tales of my Aussie encounter and the bed moving and missing condom. Disapproving daughter immediately starts tutting "you had better get back and find it" she says with great drama, implying that approving daughter will not be happy!

As her friend leaves, my daughter asks me to get her a few things and I jump back in the car and drive down the road to the local shops, getting everything on her list. By now it's nearly 10.30 pm and frankly this "Cougar" is bloody exhausted. I make sure that both my daughter and the baby are settled for the night and drive home. I decide to make a clean breast of the condom story to approving daughter and she says "don't worry mum come find it tomorrow." That was a relief; I was dead on my feet.

Opening my front door I am greeted by my son (6ft 4ins with the appetite of an elephant remember) "Alright Mum? What's for dinner? I'm starving."

Sex and the Signposts
Gaynor Evans

I look at him in disbelief, its 11pm. I've been on the go all day and now I have to cook? I wearily go to the kitchen and suggest a couple of burgers, he says fine. I really must train him better! Placing them on the grill I climb the stairs dragging my feet.

Kicking off my stilettos and reaching for my dressing gown I sit down on the bed pondering the day. At least with my daughter in the hospital I can sleep in my own bed tonight. Slipping out of my skirt and pulling my top over my head I undo my bra and standing up to put my dressing gown on I catch a glimpse of myself in the mirror. Something catches my eye and I go up close to the mirror for a better look. What on earth is that? Squashed and stuck firmly to my left breast is the missing condom. Roaring with laughter and glee I peel it off and drop it in the bin. My son hearing my whooping asks me what I'm laughing at. "Nothing" I answer, stifling another giggle. I text the Aussie that I have found the offender in my bra, which he finds hilarious! I am brought back to reality as the smell of burning burgers wafts up the stairs, what a day!

Sex and the Signposts
Gaynor Evans

Chapter Eight
SEX AND THE SIGNPOSTS

Friday comes around all too quickly. Why is it that time flies by once you are over forty? Due to various work and family pressures I feel dreadful. I'm aware that I'm at breaking point and I need to de-stress and quick.

I am having the usual girl's night out with Kate. Starting at The George which was heaving as it was a warm summers evening. This is followed by Taps the Irish Bar and then Bar Form, all our usual haunts.

Drinking rather more than usual, I get very drunk very quickly and while I'm working my way through the crowd in Taps my eyes meet with a pair of gorgeous green ones. I briefly hold his gaze and think to myself Yum! Pushing my way back to my friends I remember thinking I would have to try and talk to him later. Unfortunately I didn't get a chance as I was dragged off to the next location. Lagging behind in my drunken state I suddenly walk straight passed him on the street. I stopped dead in my tracks as did he and we stare at each other. Close too he's is even more gorgeous than I first thought and I offer up a breathless hello. He takes one step in my direction and I take two in his. After a few minutes of conversation you could virtually touch the chemistry between us. As the gap between us gets smaller and smaller the kissing starts. Wow! I

Sex and the Signposts
Gaynor Evans

was away with the fairies already or maybe that was the Vodka!

My friend, realising I was missing has come back to find me and is calling me to "Come on" very impatiently Green eyes and I quickly exchange numbers and I say looking straight into those large green eyes of his "text you later." He smiled and went off in the other direction.

One hour and four vodkas later I manage to find his number and hit the right buttons. His name is Jake and without hesitating I ask him if he wants to meet up and come home with me. He says yes immediately and I arrange to meet him at the station. Ten minutes later there he is waiting for me. I check that my friend is ok and we get in a cab back to my friend Amanda's flat. Amanda is kind enough to loan me her flat when she is away as my house is like Paddington Station. In return I feed the cat Tabitha...

Jake and I are talking quickly to each other. I find out that he is twenty seven seeing him better in the light he is about 5ft 9ins tall with a mop of curly black hair and a very big smile. We are barely able to keep our hands off each other we are both very drunk and it gets very steamy! very quickly!. The cab driver is watching with interest in his rear view mirror so we compose ourselves just for a minute and leaping out of the cab we go into the flat.

Sex and the Signposts
Gaynor Evans

Once inside he starts undressing me and kissing me at the same time, tugging at my top undoing buttons and before I know it I'm there in just my underwear. We have barely made it into the lounge. I'm aware that the light is still on and being a nearly fifty something woman I am keen to get into the bedroom where I know the light is more forgiving. (The bedroom is signposted as is the kitchen the bathroom and there are a number of no smoking signs)

My friend Amanda's mum has the later stages of Alzheimer's) Jake noticing the signs is somewhat quizzical. I explain in between kissing and stroking and sharp intakes of breathe. I try to lead him into the bedroom. He pulls me back and says "wait! Let me look at your form" still holding my hand. I remember thinking, Oh god! I wish I'd turned the bloody light off and why hadn't I been to the gym more this week. I tried to relax as I was scrutinized from head to toe. "Mmmm" he said "very nice!" then went on to explain that all his other sexual experiences had been with girls his own age and they have a different look.

He was on very shaky ground here and I thought yes, different as in younger, sexier, slimmer? I was obviously his first dalliance into the world of "Mrs Robinson". Not in the least deterred he leads me into bedroom following the signs.

Sex and the Signposts
Gaynor Evans

We spend the next hour kissing, stroking, probing and exploring each other, but sadly Mr Willy does not want to play. His frustration is evident as is his embarrassment. He said he was very turned on and couldn't understand it but put it down to the copious amounts of alcohol he had drunk and I suspect maybe some cocaine.

I was my usual supportive self in these situations which don't normally happen with a Toyboy I said not to worry and maybe later. The chemistry was so strong I was happy to wait and I know men well enough to know that the moment they have had some sleep even a little, their little friend shoots skyward completely out of their control.

So we cuddle up and sleep for about an hour when suddenly he was upon me stirring me from my sleep. I realise that the little bit of sleep has worked its magic and he was very hard indeed. He took me immediately. No foreplay or ceremony. He had something to prove. It was hot! He pulled me down the bed as if I was six stone and lifted my legs across his shoulders. Thrusting into me over and over again he was like a thing possessed. I so aroused. Moaning loudly and very wet. My noises excited him more and he became even more frantic asking me if I liked it?. "Yes" I said. "Yes" he said, "yes" I said.

This agreeing went on for some time. Shifting position slightly he suddenly put both my legs on

Sex and the Signposts
Gaynor Evans

one shoulder and then folded them in front of his body…pounding away the whole time it was intense and powerful and I loved it even if I did feel like an upside down Buddha.!!

Stopping suddenly he flipped me over and took me from behind, pounding deep into me I cried out with the painful pleasure that this position brings and then slapping me hard across my buttocks he releases me and flips on my back again, enters me once more making me gasp and resumes the kissing. He demands that I give him my tongue which he sucks into his mouth gently. He is so excited by this that he comes in a rush and we collapse in a heap.

It was getting light outside as dawn breaks and we fall asleep but not for long. In one fail swoop he stirs again and leaps on top of me, taking my breath away, kissing and licking me until my legs open and he plunges his fingers in and is spurred on by how wet I am already.

Taking his fingers out, he replaces them with his rock hard cock. Riding me gently for a few minutes he suddenly withdraws climbs up my body and offers his cock to my mouth. I happily lick it like a lollipop sucking it gently. He is groaning loudly and pulling me down the bed he lifts up my legs and enters me very strongly and pounds in and out of me until I am crying out he starts muttering yeah, yeah, yeah - over and over.

Sex and the Signposts
Gaynor Evans

Suddenly he stops leaving me feeling empty and abandoned. Pulling me to my feet and standing directly in front of the mirror that runs the whole of one side of the bedroom he places us so we can see our reflection. He pushes me gently to my knees in front of him I resume licking and sucking his cock taking it all in my mouth and out again. He was really in charge of me at this point and I was enjoying it. "Lick my balls" he demanded! I did as I was told enjoying the power play. Playing with his cock the whole time I was aware that he was watching all this in the mirror. He starts to moan loudly rocking back and forth until he explodes all over my neck and chest. Enjoying the way the warm cum felt, dripping onto me I immediately take his cock back into my mouth and gently lick and suck the remains. This cleaning up seem to be a huge turn on for guys in general and the fact I don't rush for a tissue and am happy to rub it in or leave it also excites them. I certainly would not have considered such a thing in my youth and I do seem to be much more in touch with my sexual self these days. It's quite a revelation.

We creep back into bed and fall asleep immediately to the sound of the birds singing. He wakes up with a start about 9 o'clock and goes to the bathroom (also signposted).Coming back he is looking anxious and running his hands through his gorgeous dark curls He says "I feel terrible". "Oh! Why hun?" I ask, already guessing the answer. Looking

Sex and the Signposts
Gaynor Evans

sheepish he says "I've got a girlfriend". I said "Oh ok." Thinking to myself "and your point is?" Not my problem and I wasn't expecting to see him again. Out of politeness I ask "how long have you been together?" "Two years" he's says and "I've never been unfaithful before, I'm feeling really bad now." Realising what he was saying he said "of course it's not your fault." I should think bloody not!

He said he had to go and get where he ought to be. I was still sprawled on the bed. Sitting down and leaning over he kisses me with passion. Taking my face in his hands he looks onto my eyes and says with feeling "I'm glad I met you" and then kissing me very gently once more he leaves, slamming the door behind him.

Letting out a deep sigh I lay for a while feeling languid and satiated, almost purring like a cat. Pondering the events of the night, I can still feel his hands on my body and his tongue in my mouth and despite all my best efforts I cannot feel badly about it. I stretch slowly and realise that I am now totally stress free. I snuggle into the duvet which smells of him and his aftershave and lay contentedly for a while. I am woken from my lethargy by my mobile phone it's my daughter "Mum where are you"? She demands the disapproval clearly evident. Ah well back to reality.

Sex and the Signposts
Gaynor Evans

Chapter Nine
CATCH 22

I was enjoying my Saturday. So far, I had been to the gym for a work out and a nice swim in the outdoor pool. I was trying hard to keep the 'bod' in some sort of shape now that it was being scrutinised by guys in their twenties with 20\20 vision to match! I still had a long way to go, but at least I was stopping it all heading any further south than it already had, and I was looking forward to going out later. It made a nice change not to have the usual hangover on a Saturday. I had decided not to go out last night as I was still recovering from a nasty virus that had laid me low for over a week and which had also gone through the family like a dose of salts. Other than that, on the whole, I was feeling pretty good about life.

I put the kettle on to make tea and my phone bleeped at me, reminding me that it needed charging. I plugged it in next to the kettle as it wouldn't do to have it die on me as I never know when I'm going to receive a saucy text from one of my boys. I had no sooner gone upstairs with my tea when I heard my phone ringing strains of 'Neo' wafting up the stairs. I ran back down but didn't get there quickly enough. I look to see who had called me, and see I have a missed call from No! It can't be, not the Aussie? How unusual, a text was his normal means of communication, a phone call was unheard of, and on a Saturday too! I tried to redial,

Sex and the Signposts
Gaynor Evans

but was all fingers and thumbs, and my heart was pounding. What could he want? Maybe to come up and see me this afternoon, now that would be yummy! I tried to redial again and my phone beeped to let me know that a voice message had been left. Then he rang me again and I cut him off by mistake! God this was annoying and then I finally managed to control my fingers and to redial, and this time I got to hear his lazy Aussie drawl. "How are you?" I reply "I'm good thanks" and not being able to contain myself, I cut straight to the chase "So what do I owe the honour of a phone call? Not like you!"

Instead of "are you free this afternoon?" I hear "Erm, don't know how to tell you this, it's bad news I'm afraid." My mind was racing, is he going back to Australia? He's met a girl and won't be able to see me anymore! His voice is wavering as I hear "I've recently been diagnosed with Chlamydia." I try and not let him hear my sharp intake of breath, he continues unabated. "Erm, as we had sex without a condom last time we met I thought it was only fair to tell you" I was trying to assimilate the information - Chlamydia? Are you joking? Oh Christ! I was thinking. Then I had a flash back to our last meeting, a lazy warm Saturday afternoon. Lots of steamy hard rampant and VERY unprotected sex!

Usually both absolutely fanatical about using condoms we had only decided to go 'bareback' as

Sex and the Signposts
Gaynor Evans

we had been seeing each other on a regular basis. He said that like a lot of men condoms desensitised things for him but always careful he had religiously used them for the last two years (since his long term relationship ended). My attitude had been more relaxed as I couldn't get pregnant and we agreed it would be nice to go 'Au Natural'. We said that we would each be the others exception to the rule of 'no condoms, no fun'. But I had had one or two moments! I said all the right things, not to worry and that I hadn't had any symptoms and I knew all about it and it was only really a problem in woman hoping to conceive. Definitely not a problem for me - far too bloody old! He told me that he had taken a course of antibiotics and was fine and thanked me for being so understanding but suggested I might want to have the simple test.

I do love this man, so determined to do the right thing, even if it includes making an embarrassing phone call to his much older lover. I reassured him that I had been checked out six months ago (after my first flurry of mad revenge sexual encounters) and had been clear but I would go again. And then it occurred to me. He hadn't said anything but if he was telling the truth about the two year thing then he could have caught it from me! The idea shocked me and I said as much to him. He was now reassuring me! "Don't worry, it's all fine now" but I wasn't listening. I mumbled something about "hope it hasn't put you off coming to see me" and he said "of course not" so we said our goodbyes and

Sex and the Signposts
Gaynor Evans

promised to see each other soon.

I stood in the kitchen in a state of disbelief, the realisation dawning that I was a middle aged woman that could have bloody Chlamydia an S.T.D! This was too much to take in stone cold sober, so I opened the fridge and took out the cold bottle of Chardonnay that was calling to me and poured a large glass. It may be only 2pm in the afternoon but this was an emergency. I scrambled through my bag and pulled out a squashed packet of cigarettes. I only smoke here and there and this was definitely a 'there' moment. Oh God! What if it was me? How awful, and then I kept thinking back to an occasion just before the steamy afternoon with the Aussie, when I had a chance encounter with an old flame. We had had what you would call a 'quickie' and there was barely time to get my knickers off let alone a condom on! He was married and not a player (well not much of one). Maybe he'd given it to me? And then there was the issue of If I have it, who else do I tell? Anyway it's official, I am a Tart!

My mind was working overtime and I whipped out the laptop and Googled 'Chlamydia'. I gobbled up the information and tried to see if I was symptomatic. I had been ill with this virus but that didn't match the symptoms, according to Google. Why do these things always happen at the weekend when you can't get to the Doctor?! I wouldn't be happy until I had been tested and taken the

Sex and the Signposts
Gaynor Evans

antibiotics. I kept telling myself that I probably didn't have it, although I did have a bit of an itch, but I thought that it was thrush, quite common after a bout of illness. The only plus was that as I'd been ill, I hadn't been out or been on any 'dates' and in any event I had been using condoms, so would not have passed it on.

I spent an anxious weekend and rang the Doctor first thing Monday. I asked if I could have an emergency appointment. The very efficient receptionist asked me what the nature of my problem was. Trying to sound blasé, I blurted out that I had reason to believe I may have an STD. Great! I had a vision of her making a mental note to check me out when I came in. "Could I have your date of birth please" more embarrassment as I said to her, squirming, "Do you have to have it?" She laughed and said "Don't worry - we don't pay any attention to these things". I said "Good!" and she laughed and said "But I will now!" Laughing as I gave it to her, she booked me in to see the nurse in an hour's time.

The nurse was brusque and to the point. If my 'partner' had it, then there was a good chance that I did too. Had he been treated? "Well yes, and he's not really my partner, erm, I had a phone call" I said lamely. I felt like a child caught with her fingers in the sweetie jar! Nursey had looked at me and made assumptions. She said not to worry as it was a minor bacterial infection but this was sooo

Sex and the Signposts
Gaynor Evans

embarrassing! Then she asked "What do you do for contraception?" More embarrassment followed while she scrutinised the screen, realising I was too old for that sort of advice!

She gave me a swab to do in the loo, that was a relief, at least I didn't have to put up with the KY jelly, the rubber gloves and the request to the "open wide please" followed by the insertion of the 'instrument' that every woman dreads. She handed me a prescription for three small antibiotics, and told me to hand the swab into the receptionist. Lovely!

I took the tablets as soon as I got back to the office. They gave me galloping diarrhoea and made me feel sick. But at least I knew it was seeing off the disease real or imaginary. I phoned for the results on Friday. I was positive. Oh My God, I had had it! How bloody awful! I must be the oldest swinger in town and I was left with the question of whether he gave it to me or even worse, I gave it to him. Realising that I would never know the answer, I comforted myself with the fact that at least I was in the clear now. But it had been a lesson learned, so I purchased the biggest box of condoms I could find and stuffed them in every handbag, pocket, and drawer that I owned. From now on I was going to be a girl scout and come prepared.

The following week I read an article about the rise in STDs in the older age group. This was due,

Sex and the Signposts
Gaynor Evans

apparently to people becoming single again and reliving their youth. Now you tell me ! Those nasty little germs don't care how old you are it would seem.

Sex and the Signposts
Gaynor Evans

Chapter Ten
CONFUSED.COM

It's Friday again and it's been a long, long week. Kate and I go to the town and as usually we are giving it large, large vodkas that is! By the time we reach the Irish bar we are slaughtered and head straight to the dance floor and make some serious shapes. Having checked out the talent (there wasn't any) we head off to the next bar which is a much darker place and plays alternative music. As usual it's heaving but we have no trouble getting in as the doorman (a gorgeous moonlighting fireman) knows us well and we always have a cuddle and a kiss before we go in. Kate has a soft spot for him and he often lifts her off her feet, which she loves.

We go to the bar and spot a few familiar faces and I pass the time of day with the owner who is heavily pregnant and I suggest she ought to be resting. Drinks in hand we push through the heaving throng and Kate nudges me as she spots the son of a family friend of mine. "Look" she whispers "Sean, CORR!! He's a sort!" We knew him well from various family gatherings, he was a good deal younger than Kate but had blossomed into a handsome young man with incredible shoulders and had just become Soldier, always guaranteed to get the pulse racing. We had all been at a family wedding recently. So we sauntered over and have a chat about the Bride and Groom.

Sex and the Signposts
Gaynor Evans

He was with a guy I didn't recognise and he was introduced as Nick. Nick and I chat happily about this and that and we seem to hit it off. Our discussion gets quite deep and meaningful. My brain is fuddled with vodka and I am enjoying the banter but I can't make out if we are flirting or not. He has a nice face, pleasant, hazel eyes and thick dark hair and is very cheeky. I'm not sure I fancy him but the attention is flattering. I also have the advantage because at this stage he doesn't know I'm Kate's mother. Always a bonus as I said it's a dark bar and I am usually the oldest person in there. I used to worry about this at first, but with the help of my local beauty salon and some clever clothes I tend to blend in quite nicely. It is obvious that I am older but the question of how old is cleverly sidestepped if the subject ever comes up. I am still amazed that I can pull it off but it seems I can.

Suddenly Nick leans over and whispers in my ear "Shall we get out of here?" Followed by "I like you". I ponder this statement for all of ten seconds and then say well maybe in a minute. It was only just past midnight and that really would be early doors. I was also considering the fact that he belongs to a crowd that's slightly out of bounds (friends son etc) Although I don't know this boy he knows a lot of people that know me and I can hear the gossip in my head already. They would have a field day if anything comes from this chance meeting.

Sex and the Signposts
Gaynor Evans

He is persistent and repeats "let's go right now, to my place". I'm still not sure whether we are just chewing the cud or whether he has chewing my cud in mind! Impulsively, I decide to go, the vodka assuaging my reservations. I check that Kate is in the safe hands of Sean and telling our friend the doorman to keep an eye on her we leave.

The cab station just across the street is not busy and we jump in a car. The cab drivers are always eastern European or Asian and as we get settled in our seats Sean start talking to the driver in what sounds like Punjabi. I am amazed, which I imagine was his intention. He then starts telling me that he has spent some time in India.

His place turns out to be a mobile home some distance away, near Potters Bar. We go in and he shows me round, which didn't take long! He is chattering madly and takes me through to a small balcony which overlooks fields and a vast expanse of sky. He suddenly spouts "I'd like to see the sunrise with you" a brave attempt at romance. SO! We are flirting! I can't believe I'm still second guessing it.

As I sit down on the sofa he sits next to me and then the kissing starts. Hmm pleasant but not mind blowing and I'm not sure I'm feeling this guy. The kissing (one of my fortes) seems to awaken his desire and before I know what's happening he is on his knees in front of me pushing my skirt up. He

Sex and the Signposts
Gaynor Evans

says with desperation "I want to lick you" His hand slides up my thighs and he adjusts my skimpy thong and pulling me forward he dives in head first. He laps away like a cat with a saucer of milk and I go with it losing myself in the sensations and moaning softly to encourage him. I was just thinking to myself that he knows his stuff when suddenly he stops and he emerges from under my skirt with a troubled look on his face. He tells me that he has just split up with his girlfriend of four years and this was his first sexual experience outside the relationship. "Erm maybe we shouldn't do this" - he stutters. "That's fine" - I say reassuring "Would you like a cup of tea?" he says brightly - hot sex? cup of tea? Oh well! Looks like I'm not going to find out what colour his underpants are after all.

The kitchen is in full view of the sofa and he potters about banging cups and spooning spoons and seems to be trying to distract himself. Then he stops turns to stare at me and says "I could really come over there and fuck you senseless" Bloody Hell! make your mind up! I thought we weren't doing this! The boy is confused.com. It occurs to me that I don't think I'm bothered and the tea was beginning to get my vote when he strides across the floor (all of two steps, mobile home remember!) and starts kissing me passionately. Hmmm now I am getting excited and aroused and so is he. Suddenly he starts fumbling with his jeans .Ooh! I am going to see what he keeps in his pants after all, my anticipation rising. Then he unleashes it OMG! It is a whopper.

Sex and the Signposts
Gaynor Evans

Very wide and quite long and now in my face!

I am still sitting so he offers if to my mouth, hoping. It seems rude to refuse and I immediately take it in my mouth sucking it hard, mind you it wasn't easy it was so big! He was struggling to stay upright his jeans are still round his ankles...Holding it in one hand and having had a full inspection I'm thinking that I really would like to sit on this baby...so I bring up the subject of condoms. Shaking his head he says "I don't have any." "I may have one" I answer (I usually carry some in every bag since my unfortunate experience) leaning down with one hand and still poised with his erection in my other I root through my bag. Thinking I bloody hope I've got one. With a great sense of relief, I find the purple packet hiding in the bottom. So with the trusty condom at the ready I smile and offer it to him. He looks at it shaking his head again. "It won't fit" he says with conviction "Really?" I thought they were supposed to stretch over anything. Smiling and really quite determined to have my way with this magnificent beast, I say "let's try" and I open it and start rolling it over the top of his penis, I'm getting good at this bit but after getting it down to about a third I'm struggling. They don't tell you about this in condom school!

He looks down at it and starts to help me. He manages to get it down a few more millimetres and thats it. Seems he was right. He looks at me hopefully "that will do wont it?" I inspect it again

Sex and the Signposts
Gaynor Evans

two thirds of it was in. "Yes" I say breathlessly and he flops on the sofa and I sit astride him lowering myself on to 'the beast'. It fills me up and feels amazing, but I'm still not sure we have enough chemistry. We change positions and he takes me from behind. It feels so enormous like this that it is hard to stay put and the pain is almost out weighing the pleasure, but not quite. Luckily he comes quickly and then apologises. I say its fine and after all, he did have a condom cutting off his blood supply! Getting dressed he resumes his tea-making and I'm thinking to myself that it was nice but not 'Up there' there is a lot to be said for chemistry.

At this point he starts muttering that we really shouldn't have done that. He really is beginning to get on my nerves!! Then he looks at me sideways and says "I really want to come over there and do that all again "Talk about indecisive. Thinking on my feet I say "Ah! But we can't we have no more condoms". By now my ardour (what little there had been) had cooled. He nodded in agreement and then said "I'd rather we didn't tell anyone about this" as he had come to realise we know lots of mutual people. God! He is a worrier this one. But frankly I'd rather forget all about it too.

The abandoned friends call us and we just say we are just having a cup of tea and a chat. It quite plausible as his friend knows I'm a friend of his mothers. Kate and Sean have a much more exciting night than us but that's another story! I feel the need

Sex and the Signposts
Gaynor Evans

to leave and calling a cab and kissing the somewhat confused Nick goodbye very quickly, off I go.

Kate and I have the usual post-mortem on our night out the next morning, nursing our hangovers. And logging on to my laptop I bring up the pictures of the wedding we had all been to. And staring me straight in the face is a picture of me and Nick standing next to each other and I hadn't even noticed him. Maybe that's the way it should have stayed, definitely not my finest hour!

Sex and the Signposts
Gaynor Evans

Chapter Eleven
THE IRISH EYES ARE SMILING

As the year progressed, the ways of internet dating had become second nature to me. I was now on two websites, Toyboywarehouse.com of course and a free one called Plenty of Fish. I had similar profiles on both, so my requirement for the younger man was obvious. It took a lot of time, answering messages and talking on msn to a variety of suitors.

Early on in the year I had been receiving messages from a tall dark and handsome young Irishman. He looked gorgeous and sounded even better. We had a couple of long telephone conversations and I realized that I was a sucker for the Irish accent. It positively made my toes curl. I was very keen to meet this one but we had a big problem, he was studying in Manchester.

The texts were frequent and entertaining, he had a way with words and despite never having met him, and he had got under my skin. Without any warning the texts suddenly stopped. I guess it was inevitable and I had plenty of others to keep me amused and having text him a few times with no response I deleted his name and number from my phone, presuming he had got bored.

One Saturday morning, some three months later when I was recovering from my night with Jake of the green eyes, I received a text from an unknown

Sex and the Signposts
Gaynor Evans

number. Whoever it was sent their apologies for having lost touch and sighted distance as the reason and then went on to say that he was now living and working in Spain for the holidays and would I like to go out and spend the weekend with him. I had no idea who it was being extremely hungover and unable to reason, I just sent back "who is this". The immediate reply came back lol! It's Patrick from TBW. I smiled inwardly, he was back! The texts resumed and were both romantic and sexual. The invite nice as it was, fell on stony ground, I hadn't the money and I would be far too nervous to fly out on my own to meet a stranger, tempting as it was. But our affair continued by text and the odd drunken phone call from Spain. He promised to come and see me when he returned in September. I really hoped he would. He had really got me this one. I perceived that it was very odd to feel so close to someone I'd never met. But the possibility of him was tantalizing and tempting and stretched out before me. Our texts were mutually loving and sexually charged and I have kept most of them somewhere.

September came and went and he didn't appear and with a sinking heart I realised that he probably never would. Then a text came saying that he had got involved with a girl and although still desperate to see me (he couldn't get me out of his head apparently) he was torn. I made it easy for him and said not to worry and if things changed to get back in touch.

Sex and the Signposts
Gaynor Evans

Moving swiftly on, I was excited to receive a message on POF from another young Irishman, Danny. We progressed quickly to phone calls and there it was again that sexy lilting Irish accent. I realised he was very young and he was at least two hours away on the train.

He didn't see this as a problem at all. There is something very nomadic about the Irish. He was keen to meet and on impulse one day having nothing better to do I agreed on an afternoon date. I offered to pick him up from the station and suddenly there he was banging on my car window. He looked very sweet but my goodness he did look young despite sporting some stubble. Feeling somewhat thrown by his embryonic appearance I quickly recovered myself and drove off making small talk. He was charming and had plenty to say and all in the soft Irish brogue of course. He did seem a little nervous and kept laughing a little too hard. We spent a nice couple of hours finding out about each other and he told me he had dated an older woman before but decided he didn't fancy her.

The signals were that he did fancy me. It was soon time to drop him back and I had almost decided that I probably wouldn't take it any further and then he kissed me. I was surprised and drew back to look him in the eye. We were standing and he was very tall and well built and he made me feel quite dainty

Sex and the Signposts
Gaynor Evans

(which I'm not). He held my gaze and this time I kissed him with a lot of passion to see what he would do. He kissed me right back and took charge and it seemed he had been practicing. Whoa! My stomach had wings.

You can tell lot from a kiss and it's either a big turn on or a big turn off! If it doesn't feel right it never will. Once we became unglued I mumbled something about "that was a surprise" He looked down at me with a stupid grin on his face. Composing myself I ushered him out of the door and took him back to the station.

I was now in a quandary; his texts indicated he was keen for a return visit. I liked him, he was engaging, a deep thinker and had lots of good and stimulating conversation. I wish he was a bit older but at least this was one Irishman that would turn up.

Some weeks later I found myself unexpectedly in possession of an empty flat and fancied some company. It was already 6pm in the evening; I had a vivid recollection of the kiss in my head. Testing the water, I sent him a text saying that I had an empty flat and what a shame I hadn't known earlier. The immediate reply said "I could be there in a couple of hours". I sent back "Let me think about it for a bit". Thirty minutes later I told him to come.

Sex and the Signposts
Gaynor Evans

He came bearing chocolates and a broad smile, after quizzing him about his previous experiences (I wanted to make sure there was some) we ended up in the bedroom. We discovered a lot about each other that night and the discovery was not only VERY unexpected, it was a joy to behold and was to be repeated over and over again. At last the Aussie had some competition!!

Sex and the Signposts
Gaynor Evans

Chapter Twelve
HOTTER THAN MY DAUGHTER

During my daily obsession with checking in with TBW to see who had sent me a message or a wink, I noticed an advert asking for 'Mothers who socialize with their daughters and share their clothes for a new TV show for BBC3' I thought to myself well, that would be me! I excitedly read the rest of it and deciding that I fitted the criteria I sent the researcher an email. I got a call back very quickly and we had a long discussion. She asked me loads of questions about my lifestyle and my daughters. I naturally discussed my approving daughter more as we were the ones that went out together all the time but her ears pricked up when I mentioned I had a disapproving daughter too.

The subject of toyboys came up of course and this also perked her interest. I went home chattering madly to Katie about the possibility of being in a reality TV show. As always Kate was game for a laugh and happy to take part but I was surprised when Laura said she wanted **in** as well. A few more phone calls later and Sarah (the researcher) phoned to tell me that the producer wanted us in the show. How exciting. The producer was particularly interested in the contrast between my two daughters one on my side with my lifestyle and one not, this was the hook, that and my interest in toyboys of course. They hadn't decided on a name for the show as yet but it was based on make-over format and

Sex and the Signposts
Gaynor Evans

one of us would be given a 'new look'. I had to send over photos and it would seem my whole wardrobe was going to come under scrutiny. This was just what I needed, something new to get my teeth stuck into; the single life wasn't so bad after all!

The filming was to start in November and the show would be screened in February 2010, Sarah rang me to tell me they had come up with a name and so 'Hotter than my Daughter' was born. I can't say I was overjoyed at the name; I was not arrogant enough to suggest that in any way that statement was true of me. As far as I was concerned both my daughters where beautiful in very contrasting ways. Laura was more natural and had great bone structure; Kate was more glamorous and had inherited my great red hair. Kate loved dressing up and Laura loved dressing down so the make-over team would have their work cut out.

My life became very busy, I was still trying to keep my recruitment business afloat under very hard times luckily my boss a lovely man, was cutting me plenty of slack and I was very busy with the family and of course my toyboys. I had a few new ones in the loop but my favourite the Aussie was still visiting when he could and Danny was becoming a firm fixture in my diary now. **He** was definitely growing on me. Tactile and sweet he makes best use of his kissable lips in all the right places. He hangs on my every word and tells me that I am gorgeous

Sex and the Signposts
Gaynor Evans

and my eyes aren't just blue they have three different colours in them and all this in his soft Irish accent. He makes me tea and has the sexual stamina of an athlete. When people ask me "Why toyboys?" the answers are endless and all very good for me.

However, trying to fit everything in was hard but I loved being in the middle of this whirlwind. My dates with Danny had to be squashed in around his Uni work and the flat or my house being available. I was constantly trying to juggle everything and with him keen to visit again I took a half days holiday and we went to Katie's flat for the afternoon. This would be the fourth time I had seen him and I was really looking forward to it. The sex was getting better and better, we just seemed to have a connection and the chemistry was so strong it was almost tangible.

It was late afternoon by the time we slipped into the bedroom and began to play. It was getting dark outside and we were cosy and warm but my phone would not stop ringing the researchers, wanting to book filming dates in, the office, my friends. I was laying naked on the bed with the phone pressed firmly to one ear and Danny lying beside me. He was waiting patiently, kissing my breasts, my neck and stroking my body and my face whilst I take call after call. In the end I switched off the phone and gave him my full attention.

Sex and the Signposts
Gaynor Evans

I lay in the half-light flat on my back, with the weight of his gorgeous body on top of me as he takes me over and over again. I am totally lost and I am so aroused, all my senses are connecting at once, from my head to my toes. I almost reach orgasm more than once and this would have been a first. I am blown away by this boy's capacity to control himself. We have been like this now for some time and I am desperate for release and know that he will have to use his tongue to achieve this. I start muttering to him softly in between kisses and tongues meeting. "I want you to come inside me, come inside me now" He calmly looks me in the eyes and confirms "Now?" "Yes" I whisper back "now please". He obliges almost instantaneously moaning softly and covering my face in kisses.

We lay for a few minutes entwined and tangled and breathless until he works his way down my body. He snuggles his head between my thighs and proceeds to find my orgasm for me. It is laying in wait just below the surface and it only takes a few flicks of his tongue to bring it up and over. The sound of my moaning and gasping fills the room as I thrash on the bed. As orgasms go, it is enormous, huge and totally overwhelming. Once I am spent and my body is back to a quiet calm he moves slowly upwards kissing me every step of the way. He reaches my face and we kiss some more our tongues meeting. I stroke his face with my fingers looking into his deep green eyes. Smiling at him I say simply 'Wow'.

Sex and the Signposts
Gaynor Evans

He smiles back and is very pleased with himself. So he should be, I am no stranger to sex (obviously) but that was on a whole different level and I tell him as much. We cuddle up for a while as the darkness of the grim November evening closes in on the flat and realising we need to get out before Kate returns from work. I begin to get dressed and switching my phone back on (it starts ringing immediately) I get yet another call from the TV show changing a filming date. It is quite hard for us all to be available on the same day but we are all essential to the proceedings.

Elated and relaxed I fill Danny in on the latest update on the show as I drive him to the station and we agree that he must come again soon, and I'm hoping that next time I can arrange for him to stay over. I really must have some more of that!!

The researchers for the show having spoken to us all individually want to start the filming on a Thursday. The plan is to film me first going through my wardrobe and me modelling some of the clothes I wear when I'm out. They were particularly interested in a pair of white denim hot pants that I had mentioned on the phone. I had first worn these on holiday when we had gone to the beach and then out clubbing and I had sent them a photo of me in them. So parading around my bedroom wearing them and a pair of wedge sandals on a cold November afternoon seemed to be the order of the day.

Sex and the Signposts
Gaynor Evans

I changed clothes a few times and they took film and stills of me in everything. In between they interviewed me about my lifestyle and of course endless questions about the toyboys. I was careful not to mention any names; I referred to the boys by their country of origin and didn't give too much away. I had realized early on that the boys were pretty covert about their activities into the world of the 'Mrs Robinsons' and I wouldn't want to blow their cover inadvertently. I was also terrified that I would get an irate mother on my doorstep welding a rolling pin and accusing me of seducing and corrupting her son. It was a scene I had often replayed in my head.

After lunch my daughters arrived and they were interviewed individually and then together and we had lots of picture taken. The plan was that we would go into the city for a proper night out to one of our regular haunts 'Revolution' accompanied by the film crew. The wine was opened early and by the time we got in the car we were all feeling very jolly. Lady Gaga was playing loudly on the radio and in the back all three of us sang along loudly, completely out of tune. They had to get permission to film in the club and it was surprising how many wine bars refused to allow them to. By now we were all very comfortable with the crew and just acted as if they weren't there. We danced and chatted up any passing punter and they filmed it all. How much of this would end up on the cutting room

Sex and the Signposts
Gaynor Evans

floor we didn't know but it was too late to worry about that now.

The next day's filming was planned in for a Sunday. The presenter of the show Liz McClarnon of Atomic Kitten fame was coming to the house and it would take all day. We were all very excited and I whisked about tidying the house and making preparations.

What to wear was of paramount importance of course and I settled for my long boots and little red skirt. When Liz arrived there was various takes before she actually entered the house and a lot of hanging about. She was charming very down to earth and easy to get on with, the filming went without a hitch. The plan seemed to be to highlight the different points of views held by my two daughters with regards to my dress sense and my toyboys.

At one point when Liz asked the girls. "So, who's hotter then you or your mum?" A row almost broke out between them as they both had very different views on that subject. But it all made good TV. As for me when repeatedly asked the same question I would side step it neatly. The filming took a long time but was enjoyable and with just a day to do in the studios and the make-over's to look forward too we could relax a bit.

By now it was December and with Christmas fast

Sex and the Signposts
Gaynor Evans

approaching my life was even more frantic than usual. There was the Christmas shopping to do and the planning for the 'big day', then lots of invitations, dinners and party nights and of course toyboy dates to fit in. Our last day of filming was booked in for Sunday the 20th of December. We were the last family to have the make-over. We travelled into Liverpool Street where a cab picked us up and took us to the studio a tiny mews house which they called 'Hotness heaven'. We were welcomed by the now familiar crew and given wine and lunch whilst everything was made ready. We still had absolutely no idea who was getting the makeover out of the three of us as this would have depended on the public vote. We were all very excited and looking our best, we had to do cat walk modelling whilst being filmed in various poses. It all felt a bit strange and I struggled to walk in my thigh high boots that I had opted to wear, stupidly.

But eventually once the nerves had settled they got the poses they wanted and we were taken into the studio for the filming. The room was covered in large pictures of famous mothers and daughters Goldie Hawn and Kate, the Paris Hiltons, Kelly and Sharon Osbourne. Liz was waiting and we stood nervously in front of her. We had been told she would be asking us various questions but we didn't know what they would be. She immediately addressed me and grinning she asked me "had I heard the word Cougar?" Generally, us older woman hate the word cougar as it makes us sound

Sex and the Signposts
Gaynor Evans

like predatory animals and is not very flattering. She then defined the word Cougar saying it was a woman of forty years or older that sexually pursues men of eight years her junior or younger. I immediately defended my position and the other 'Mrs Robinsons' out there by saying that we didn't gang haul them into it and in the main they pursued us.

She then moved swiftly on to the public vote starting with me. They showed me the large life size picture that they had taken out on the street to get opinions on. It was me in the shorts of course, they must have wanted as much controversy as possible, but I was horrified it was without doubt the ugliest and most horrendous picture of me that I had ever seen. They had taken countless nice pictures of me and then decided to use this terrible one and what was worse it had been paraded out in public and was now on national television. My heart sank I had been well and truly stitched up and I had a feeling that there would be more of the same to come. Joe Jury (the public) were very vocal about my attire and one member made the comment "Worst than mutton dressed as lamb" charming. I handle this remark with humour and then Liz turned her attention to Kate 'Tarty' Laura 'No character'. Keeping us on tender hooks she announced with a flourish that the make-over was going to Laura. Kate and I cheered and then she looked at me and said, "AND Gaynor" pausing for effect.

Sex and the Signposts
Gaynor Evans

I was dumbfounded I didn't realise that there was a possibility two of us would be made over. Kate whooped and jumped in the air realising, she had been let off the hook. Laura and I were separated and led to different rooms where the changes began.

Hair was first. They decided to colour mine and at some point Laura and I were both bundled into a cab sporting towels on our head and still blind folded and taken to a salon in the middle of a busy Christmas shopping London. What a sight we must have looked. They wouldn't let us talk or see each other. Back in the cab and back to the studio make up was next. I got the impression from the team they were going to give me a softer look this worried me.

As I had stated earlier I was big on make-up and I loved false eyelashes and was never seen without my slap. My pale redheaded colouring meant that without make up I looked like a blank canvass. I chattered nervously to the make-up artist expressing my fears and she reassured me that she was going to make me another sort of beautiful. Hmm I wasn't convinced but just had to go along with it.

Finally came the clothes, they stepped me into various outfits, still blind folded of course. I could feel material and get an idea but that's all. My feet were squashed into all sorts of shoes. Two or three assistants fussed and flapped around me and I had the indignity of being laced into some spandex 'hug

Sex and the Signposts
Gaynor Evans

me in' underwear (Gok Wan would have approved). It may make your outline look smooth and defined but I wouldn't be seen dead in it. It was about as sexy as a bin bag!! Eventually the team stood back and announced that's it. The new 'me' was complete.

I had still not seen myself and had no idea how I looked. I was taken back into the studio and placed behind a white screen and told to wait for my cue. The fashion team murmured reassuring and soothing words, you look beautiful, amazing, and lovely. I was still very worried about the make-up; I hadn't been seen in public without my eyelashes for some time. Let alone in front of thousands of TV viewers.

Liz, Kate, and Laura were all waiting behind the screen for me to make my grand entrance. I walk boldly out and try and take in the view. Standing beside a huge covered mirror is Liz with Kate still in her sparkly red dress; I don't immediately recognize the person next to Kate and then realise it is in fact my daughter, Laura. My god! She looked different, her hair had gone from blonde to jet black she was in a bright coloured dress greens and blues and she was wearing false eyelashes and loads of make-up and frankly looked unrecognisably stunning.

Their attention was then turned on me. I was worried Kate looked perturbed. Liz asked the

Sex and the Signposts
Gaynor Evans

question "what do you think of your mum?" Laura used the word "understated" Kate backed her up with "Very understated". I was guessing that 'understated' was not good and my heart sunk. Kate qualified the point "she looks like Helen Mirren" The reason this comment was so significant was that when the researchers had asked Kate who I would aspire to look like they had offered up Helen as a suggestion. Kate had given them a very firm and emphatic NO!! Don't get me wrong 'Helen Mirren' is gorgeous and a brilliant actress but she is a subtle beauty. There is absolutely nothing subtle about me.

Now extremely anxious to see myself Liz offers me the 'Big Reveal' and in one sweeping gesture she pulls the cover from the mirror. I peer into it and begin to analyse my appearance. I am trying to be as positive as possible after all the team had spent a long time achieving this look. Starting from the shoes up I start talking. I like the shoes the dress although very conservative is nice enough and they have dressed it up with a sparkly belt. I do look very curvaceous and not a bulge insight courtesy of the spandex. My hair is a darker blonde and there is more of it. But my face is so understated I feel completely undressed and exposed. My skin looks nice and glowy but the lip gloss doesn't highlight my mouth and without the eyelashes and colour on my eyes they had lost them completely. They look 'piggy' and undefined. I immediately say so. Liz then asks me the leading question "Are you hotter

Sex and the Signposts
Gaynor Evans

than your daughter?" My answer is to raise the clutch bag to neck in a cutting movement and I say from the neck down, maybe. Laura and I then have to do various catwalk poses and we are done. I immediately rush back to the dressing room and rummaging through my bag I swiftly stick on my false eyelashes. The plan had obviously been to glam up Laura and to tone me down. I wasn't happy but it was too late now. I would just have to take it on the chins.

We are allowed to keep our outfits, which is nice and my dress will be useful for work. Laura was still coming to terms with her shocking transformation and Kate had had some fun having gone for a drink with a rather handsome production assistant. All in all it had been a great experience. We get cab back to the station and spend the journey home chattering madly amongst ourselves. We are looking forward to the programme airing with some trepidation.

Christmas arrives and the family descends upon me and with the Champagne flowing a great time was had by all. This is followed by nice long afternoon spent in the arms of the Aussie, and with Danny hot foot back to Ireland my sexy Australian was a welcome sight. I tell him all about the show he is amused and says with a wry smile that he will look out for it.

Sex and the Signposts
Gaynor Evans

In January the publicity machine rolls into action and I am contacted by a journalist who wants to do a story for a newspaper. I agree to an interview and we get on well. She tells me that she has the Sunday People interested and will be able to get me a small fee. Their photographer contacts me and we arrange for him to come and take some shots.

He has me posing all over the house and the garden and his final shot is one of me lying on my dining table, stretched out like a cat. It is a good job that I have a sense of the ridiculous. In the meantime they have begun to run a trailer for the show on BBC3, it is repeated over and over and there I am right at the beginning in the club dancing and chatting up a young guy. I squirm, it's a profile shot and the turkey neck is on show, and even though this is rather overshadowed by my long Roman nose URGH!! It's not a good look.

Cut to Manchester, Patrick is sitting with his girlfriend on the sofa, when the trailer comes on the TV. Nearly choking on his drink he recognises me immediately even though we have yet to meet. Guiltily he wings of a sneaky text simply asking "Babe have I just seen you on TV?" I roar with laughter TV has a long reach. I answer "yes afraid so" he texts back "I can't believe it, and feel guilty even though we haven't met yet". I can see why he would , we have had and 'affair' of sorts even if it was all done via text and phone, some of his messages were very deep and sexual and if I was his

Sex and the Signposts
Gaynor Evans

girlfriend, I would hang him for less. Anyway, I figure that as the shots of me weren't that great he was probably put off and text him accordingly. But no! He thinks I look hot and desperately still wants to meet me but is so torn. Oh dear!

The newspaper article comes out the following Sunday and I rush across to the Co-operative to buy a copy. I have told all my friends and family to look out for it and I am quite excited by the prospect of reading my story. I had been told that it would be in the small magazine supplement that comes with the paper. I look through it page by page no sign of me. Surely it's not in the paper and I start looking, It is **very** easy to find, an enormous two page spread with a picture of me in colour covering both pages and the heading "I ditched my cheating husband and now I'm a Cougar like Courtney (Cox)".In big letters to the side of the picture are the words "And now I've had 25 toyboys". I had never said that! She asked me how many dates I'd been on with toyboys and qualified it with "more than 25?" I had answered yes, but to dates, not bedpost notches. That's it then, I am now officially and publically a slapper.

I was going to show the article to my mum, definitely out of the question now. I felt exposed and had the urge to go and buy up every copy. Some of the facts were also incorrect but that was the least of my worries. I now know why Celebrities get so fed up with journalists. What is it they say?

Sex and the Signposts
Gaynor Evans

There's no such thing as bad publicity!

The week our episode is due to air I get a phone call from one of my colleagues at our other office in Luton. Giggling loudly she says have I looked on you tube? Obviously I hadn't, barely able to get the words out she says "I think you should". "What am I looking for I ask?" She says spluttering "Cougar loose in Enfield" Really? Oh my God!! With a wry smile on my face I type the words in Google. The clip is about two minutes long and there for the entire world to see; my guilty secret is now 'out there'. I am 'The Cougar loose in Enfield' and I eat young men for breakfast.

"It's mandatory to grow old, but it's optional to grow up"

Sex and the Signposts
Gaynor Evans

Chapter Thirteen
JUMPING JACK FLASH

As the furore surrounding the programme dies down, life became somewhat dull. The excitement of the filming and the makeovers and the publicity quickly passed. And life slips back into routine, work, home the family and the odd girls nights out. This is interspersed of course with random visits from Danny whenever he can manage it, which frankly is never often enough for me. I had recently heard from the Aussie who seems to want to keep in touch and is promising to visit me soon. Frankly I hope he does, I am becoming far too dependent on the young Irishman and can't allow myself to get in any deeper, I must be mad.

I kept my profile active on both my favourite website 'TBW' (where I found the Aussie) and 'POF' (where I found Danny). I get a lot of messages and I scrutinise the pictures thoroughly before I reply. My heading on POF clearly states that I am looking for a Devoted Toyboy but I still get the older variety chancing their arm. It wasn't uncommon for me to get a bolshie comment from gentleman in their fifties, very miffed that I only have eyes for the young and telling me that I ought to try a 'Real man' I usually treat these with the contempt they deserve only occasionally rising to the bait and sending a measured reply. It not that I wouldn't date an older man I just don't seem to find any that have the same energy and enthusiasm for

Sex and the Signposts
Gaynor Evans

life that I do. They always seem very low key, dour and riddled with talk about ailments and mistreatments and the price of everything.

They just don't seem too bring much joy to the table and for that reason and because my glass is nearly always half full I give them a wide berth. They may well want to bath in my aura but I definitely don't want to be dragged into their fading light, not when mine is still shining so brightly. Harsh I know but someone, anyone? Please prove me wrong.

I get a message from a very tall long haired young man on POF. Studying his picture I decided I quite like what I see. Strong face, bit on the long side but with very soft wide apart eyes giving him a nice open countenance. We exchange a few messages and he quickly asks for my phone number and we text for a bit and then he phones me. His name is Jack and he has the deepest voice I have ever heard it's rich and smooth and very sexy. He laughs a lot seems very genuine and tells me he has a passion for music (that explains the long hair) plays in a band and works part-time behind a bar in a restaurant.

We get on well, he seems polite and there are no overtly sexual undertones. The only drawback is that he lives in Luton which is up the motorway and so a no go area for me. We chat over a couple of evenings and he is keen to meet up and says he is quite happy to drive to me. We arrange a date,

Sex and the Signposts
Gaynor Evans

which he then cancels due to 'Man flu' As I have said many times the patience of a saint is required.

We arrange to meet at a pub that nestles in a country lane just off the motorway. This pub called The Robin Hood is an ideal venue for the clandestine meeting and I know from my girlfriends that anyone having an illicit affair often uses this as a meeting place. There is a hotel just down the road and it has some nice cosy sofas by the fire. I park at one side of the car park and he is in the other. He is on time and greets me with a big very toothy grin (will have to watch those babies later if we get to the snogging stage!) He is very tall and lean and although the hair is fairly long it is carefully arranged. He is in jeans and a jacket and looks good enough to eat. Luckily I have had dinner, I like him immediately.

He goes to the bar and asks me what I would like. He is doing well so far. We sit side by side on the sofa and the conversation is easy and I can feel the warmth building between us. He tells me that he really wants to be a musician and plays guitar and keyboards and sings a bit. He and his girlfriend have split up fairly recently and he is looking to spread his wings, he is after all the grand old age of twenty five. He lives in a rented house that he shares with one other guy. Noticing my glass is empty he jumps up and goes to the bar. I protest saying that I will buy this round, he won't hear of it and insists, I smile inwardly this guy has a lot of

Sex and the Signposts
Gaynor Evans

good points.

The evening flies by and when he escorts me to my car I suggest that he gets in with me. I laugh as he completely fills up the passenger seat with his long legs and big hair and getting quite cosy we chat some more. Fifteen minutes later and he asks me very politely if he can kiss me. Thinking I thought you'd never ask, I look into his big brown eyes and nodding I lean in. The kissing is interesting and I have to negotiate his overfull mouth. His teeth are lovely but it seems that he may have someone else's in there as well. However the chemistry is stirring and my stomach does the up and over thing and our hands touch. He has big hands but long slender guitar players' fingers and he smells delicious. He asks' me if I would like to meet up again and I say yes, he seems very pleased with this answer. He suggests that I might like to go to his place one night and chill out. This sound very nice but of course the problem of the motorway looms up. Jack is quick to reassure me that he is quite happy to come and pick me and drop me back the next day. OOOH I'm having a sleepover, what fun. But it really is very sweet of him it's a good hour's drive each way.

He gets out of my car and I watch his tall upright figure walk across the car park in the dark. He gets something from his pocket and I see his face - illuminated by the flame from a lighter as he draws on a cigarette very rock star!!! and he was

Sex and the Signposts
Gaynor Evans

obviously too polite to smoke in front of me, I drive home singing along to the Script that are warbling out from my CD player and decide that I have found my very own 'Mick Jagger' and that I am really looking forward to my sleepover.

We spend the next week or so texting and speaking on the phone and trying to arrange a suitable night for me to visit the wilds of Luton. It is proving difficult with him working all weekend and my busy schedule but we settle for the following Thursday. It isn't till some days later that Chloe reminds me that we have a long standing dinner arrangement at Maria's for the same evening. Damn It.!!

A group of us that started out in recruitment many years ago had bonded and we always meet up for dinner on an irregular basis. Everyone is in different places in their lives and organising an evening when we are all free is like a military operation. So now what? I text Jack and he is very disappointed. I'm not the sort of woman who sidelines friends for a date with man but I know what I would rather do. It occurs to me that our girls' evenings are not normally late affairs, so maybe, just maybe? I text Jack and ask how late he would be prepared to come and get me. He says he doesn't mind as he won't be working on the day. I suggest 10.30pm and he says no problem. Chloe says she is happy to drop me off and I agree to meet him in the same pub car park. I will be taking the Friday off so can have a lazy morning with him. Thursday is now looking much more promising.

Dinner at Maria's as always is superb and we have a great evening of banter and catching up. I drink a fair amount of wine and I am in high spirits. I check my phone constantly, waiting for Jacks text to say he is on his way. There is always a chance that he will go flaky. The younger man has a perchance for 'flaky behaviour' as I like to call it. Last minute cancellations, with excuses of man flu, sick grandparents or emergency visits to the vets with the family budgie. I have heard them all. It is the nature of the animal. I was relieved then to get the text telling me he was half an hour away. With the girls all expressing their concern that I was going into the unknown (I have no such reservations) With the exception of Amanda the wild child, all the others are married with young children and living settled and routine lives. Good luck to them and long may it last, for me, been there done that! And here I am on the verge of another adventure.

I jump in Chloe's car and she delivers me in the rain to the dark car park. We giggle all the way singing various Rolling Stones numbers including Jumping Jack Flash. He winks his lights to indicate his presence and I get out of the car with some wine in one hand and my bag in another. Frankly though I think I have drunk enough. I climb into his car and he sets off. The music playing loudly from his CD

Sex and the Signposts
Gaynor Evans

player I recognise immediately its 'The Doors' one of my favourite bands from the seventies and 'Riders of the Storm' one of my favourite tracks. I mention that it's rather an unusual choice for someone his age. He laughs saying that he listens to all sorts in his quest for inspiration to write and play his own songs, he is just getting into the Doors apparently. Feeling very at home and sixteen again - I sing loudly remembering every line as we whip up the motorway on our way to Bedfordshire. He stops on the way at Tesco's saying that he is hungry and wants a Pizza. I find out that needing food is a constant driving force of his. It must take a lot to feed that tall frame and I understand completely having a similar giant with the same name living at home whose head is constantly in the fridge.

His place is a nice house in a quiet street which his father owns and he rents on the cheap. He shares it with a flat mate who occupies most of the upstairs. It's nice and cosy and we open the wine and he takes me into his bedroom which has a large flat screen TV and an inviting bed. It is also full of musical instruments. He puts the pizza in the oven and we chat easily. He is easy company and I feel safe and well looked after and this tips over into feeling very rampant all of a sudden. In between mouthfuls of pizza and sips of wine we settle on the bed. My shoes are off and he flicks from programme to programme and eventually settles for some old film. He tells me all about his girlfriend and their constant arguments and I give him a few

Sex and the Signposts
Gaynor Evans

details of my marriage and the TV show that I've just done. He leaps up and immediately gets me up on YouTube. He thinks it's all good fun and I laugh along with him.

Eventually we cuddle up on the bed and we kiss long hard and with a great deal of passion. Undressing slowly we slip under the covers and we stroke and play with each other enjoying the feel of skin on skin. My hand brushes his cock it is rock hard and I slide down taking it in my mouth He reciprocates sliding between my legs licking me slowly and driving me wild and we are lost in our enjoyment of each other.

He produces a condom and slides deep inside, my god it feels wonderful. He pushes in and out of me slowly and then builds up speed until I stop him. I push him up and indicate that I would like him to lie down on the bed and I climb on top of him .I place my hands on his lean frame and slowly take him in and out of me loving every inch of him. He takes control and turns me over and pushes back inside me with ease and comes after a few strong thrusts. We flop back on the bed and he clings to me with his head on my stomach panting loudly and I stroke his long hair. We curl up kissing and then fall asleep.

As soon as we wake up we have sensuous and slinky morning sex and after lots of kissing he leaps out of bed and goes in search of breakfast. He

Sex and the Signposts
Gaynor Evans

comes back with a bowl of cereal and a cup of green tea for me with milk in YUK! But I give him 'A' for effort it's a while since anyone bought me tea in bed. We pass the morning relaxed and in easy conversation and he tells me all about his colourful family and more about his recent break up. But music is all he really cares about and I find that very refreshing.

At some point I go to the bathroom and get dressed and it's time for him to take me home. Its pouring with rain and cold and his hair is sticking up at right angles all over his head, I have attempted to flatten down my usual evidence of sex hair. He gives up with his and pulls on a blue beanie hat which has the effect of making him look younger but suits him down to the ground. No fashionable under twenty five year old is without one this year and sales must have rocketed because of the bitter winter we are having.

Once on the car the conversation continues. The motorway is slow in the rain and at one point a lorry pulls out on us and he has to swerve to avoid it. With my heart in my mouth I gasp saying to him that this is exactly why I don't do motorways. He seems to take the incident in his stride despite the fact that he had told me earlier that he had been in a bad car smash. He is definitely braver than me! We pass the pub that we had met in and he drives me to my door - struggling to find a place to park in my street as usual, he pulls over just outside and we

Sex and the Signposts
Gaynor Evans

kiss goodbye agreeing to do it again. The kissing is somewhat prolonged and a car pulls up and toots its horn, I look and realise it's my sons friends and as I look the other way I spot my son - also 6ft 4ins sporting his own beanie hat coming down the path. The similarities between the two are not lost on me, and not wanting to be caught I quickly get out of the car blowing Jack a kiss through the window. He drives away and my son whose focus was on his friends' arrival does not seem to have spotted his mother kissing his clone. Thank God for that!!

Jack and I keep in contact and I would have liked to have seen him again. He texts me a week later to tell me that his girlfriend - probably having sensed he was moving on, had pleaded with him for another chance. For the moment he was going to see how that goes. So no more Jumping Jack Flash for me but to quote the 'Stones' at least it had been a "gas, gas, gas"!

"Men do not quit playing because they grow old. They grow old because they quit playing"

Oliver Wendell Holmes

Sex and the Signposts
Gaynor Evans

Chapter Fourteen
FEELING THE FEAR

I had come to the conclusion lately that dating the younger, man is fraught with emotional danger. The moment you get into a regular arrangement whether it's once a week, once a month or anywhere in between, you are in big trouble. You start to forget the mammoth age gap when relating to your latest conquest or conquests. (Seeing more than one does give you some protection against emotionally over investing.) And expect them to behave and think the way you do. This is a big mistake, they just aren't capable of doing it and that is what makes the relationship you do have with them so exciting and intoxicating.

It develops in a sort of lopsided way, you bring to the table years of experience and baggage from your previous relationships and they bring enthusiasm, love of life, optimism and promise of the men they will become. I have found it hard in some cases not to want more and more commitment; I don't mean marriage or introducing them to your family or meeting theirs but just being there a bit more. For example, being able to ring them when you have a problem. Don't get me wrong in some cases it is possible. But the chances are they will move on to a more suitably aged mate before you can even get to the stage of intimate problem sharing and this can be painful.

Sex and the Signposts
Gaynor Evans

When I started on this experience, I thought that I would mainly have, short sex filled liaisons, maybe spanning one to six dates. Of course this did happen with some but what I hadn't expected was some of them to last for months and even into my second year of singledom. This is when it gets tricky, a relationship (lopsided) does develop and then you start to have expectations of it.

At this point you could start putting on the pressure. Moaning if they don't text back in a suitable time or not getting to see you often enough or even sidelining you for a night out with their mates. If you do, this is the beginning of the end it then takes on a different shape and stops becoming spontaneous and fun and becomes like all the other relationships you have ever had and slips into monotony and angst.

The first time I let this happen to me was in the case of my delightful Aussie. After a whole year of dating sporadically and having the most amazing sex, I realized that I had grown fond of him and made the mistake of telling him so. It was Christmas week and we had spent a languid and cosy afternoon in our usual way (fucking each other's brains out). He seemed non-plussed by this information and I had used the word 'fond' not 'love'. I wasn't in love with him; I wouldn't allow myself that indulgence as it had cost me so dear in the past. I did believe though, that had we been a similar age things could have been different. We got on in a lot of ways and the chemistry was strong, but then would it have been if we were nearer in age? Maybe it was that very fact that made it so electric. I didn't know the answers, just knew I loved his sex texts, his company and his hands on my body.

After my somewhat feeble declaration of 'fondness' I regretted it immediately, much safer not to show your hand. He mumbled something about "best to be honest". Hmmm I could see the slight sign of unease flash across his face.

A few weeks later towards the end of January, I sent him a text the usual 'Hi how are you? Any chance of a visit soon?' His reply was courteous (he is never anything but, another of his likeable qualities!) but included the words "I have met someone and we are dating and I don't think I should see you at the moment as I just want to see how it goes, sorry" My heart sank, the thought of not having him to look forward to was a blow. I replied as lightly as I could, wishing him luck and ending with if things don't work out you know where I am. He laughed, but his message was clear, he was backing off, the word 'fond' had hit home.

I knew there probably was a girlfriend, but it was also probable that he was letting me down gently. Scared I was getting too attached. I sat quietly starring at my phone and trying to work out how I felt. I phoned my friend Amanda for input, she was

Sex and the Signposts
Gaynor Evans

as usual honest, repeating her usual mantra that keeping more than one on the go was the only answer. Just as well then, that I had done just that and my gorgeous young Irishman had just returned and was keen to see me.

I was moderately bereft about the loss of my sexy Aussie, but was to find out in the months to come that the gap was filled beyond my expectations. The Aussie and I kept in loose contact and one sunny Saturday he travelled up to see me and all was as before. It hadn't worked out with the girlfriend, and he is now firmly back in the loop. Her loss is my gain it would seem, just better keep the word 'fond' out of the conversation in future!!

.

This experience did not however stop me doing it all again and with bells on. In the case of young Danny, keeping control of my emotions was to prove even more difficult and then impossible and then. Oh Crap!!

Sex and the Signposts
Gaynor Evans

Chapter Fifteen
POCKETSIZED PERFECTION

It's Sunday, a gloomy March morning. The promise of spring is everywhere, but the claws of winter are digging deep. It's raining softly and I focus on the tree outside my window where I can see tiny birds hopping about, chirping away. I think back to the other tree that I used to look at from my other window, in my other life. My how things have changed!!

I'm sitting in my bedroom, in my large king size bed writing this, the same bed that earlier this week was well and truly occupied on Monday with Steve, and Thursday with Danny. Hmmm, does the fact that there's been two bother me? Do I feel ashamed? Nope! My domestic set up is so complicated, and in order to keep my son from being totally disgusted with his mother, I have to make the most of his absences when they occur (which isn't often). The bed is dishevelled and I bury myself in the cushions breathing in the lingering smell of its occupants, which is comforting. I will be using those two days and nights to occupy and excite my thoughts this week as there is no such fun expected and the days stretch out before me without punctuation.

It occurred to me recently that I write about my toyboy encounters in order to capture and relive the moment. I know that I will be unable to hold onto

Sex and the Signposts
Gaynor Evans

these fledgling men; I might be enjoying them now but I will become a distant memory and just part of their growing pains. All I can hope for is that they retain a fond memory or two of the time we spent together and at the very least have a tale or two to regale to their friends of the time they bedded 'Stifler's Mother'. For my part the joy they bring me, short lived as it is, makes me feel desirable, sexy and alive. Frankly I count myself very lucky that I will have these memories to look back on, I had never expected to be having so much fun. Age it would seem was no barrier to attracting men of all types, and I was having the time of my life!!. And let's be honest, I had tried the long term committed relationship stuff and the joy was over quickly and the pain, both physical and mental, had been excruciating. I may be cynical, but life can do that to you, well at least from my experiences. But back to the joy!

When Steve arrives on Monday he seemed a little more reserved than I remember. Clutching his back pack (they all seem to have those and it always reminds me of school boys which is naughty). We go into the kitchen and from the aforementioned bag he produces the ingredients for tonight's dinner, which he gallantly offered to cook for me. I think that it's quite brave of him to cook for me, an older woman who has spent more years in the kitchen than he's been on the planet. We chat over a glass of wine as he prepares the food, and I find it very hard to leave him to it, in my own house.

Sex and the Signposts
Gaynor Evans

He manages it all beautifully and throws together the most delicious dish of fresh pasta and chicken in breadcrumbs with a sauce and mozzarella. We eat at the table and afterwards, with wine in hand, we go through to the lounge and sit side by side on the sofa. Having polished off a fair bit of wine, and two rather large gin and tonics, I'm rather drunk and I'm still sensing that he wants to run away. I ask quietly "Are you ok? Erm, you seem a little tense."
"I'm fine" he replies "and very relaxed." I remember at this point that during our arrangement making, he had said that he may need to go home to let a builder into his flat in the morning. I was convinced, and I still am, that this was a sort of get out of jail card. "Will you be staying?" I ask, as lightly as possible. Raising his glass in the air he smiles and says " Looks like it." Good that means I may get sex tonight and in the morning! He still hasn't kissed me yet, which is odd, because on the last two occasions we have met, he has not lost an opportunity to grab me early on and give me the benefit of his gorgeous lips.

So deciding to take control of the situation I lean over and give him one of my finest snogs. He kisses me back, really tenderly, and I feel my passion stir. The gaps between my sexual encounters can be long and maybe go on for weeks, so I find myself impatient and I want to take control and have him there and then. So clothes off! Well all, except my little La Senza 'teddy' (one of a couple I own). I like to keep this on for most of the time because it

Sex and the Signposts
Gaynor Evans

keeps my boobs up and my fat bits down. Steve is busy un-wrapping his gorgeous hard body and sitting back down on the sofa he looks up at me as I stand poised over him like a praying mantis. His eyes are amazing; deep, deep blue, wide apart and with long curly eyelashes, I could dive in them and swim around. My eyes are drawn downward to his cock, which is now also blinking at me. He is not very tall, 5ft 7ins, but is perfectly formed and as fit as a flea from endless games of squash. He has a hard firm body without an ounce of fat. He is muscular without being 'built' and is in perfect proportion. When I first had the pleasure of Steve it had been a quick but very exciting moment or two in the front of my car (Courgarmobile).

We had met for a drink and I had found him a delight. He was very demonstrative in public, kissing me in the pub and getting stuck in without any worries of who might see him with the 'old bird'. I found this very endearing and when we went back to the car, the kissing became so passionate and I was so turned on I didn't seem to have any brakes. I decided it was high time that the 'Courgarmobile' was christened. I drove quickly to a dark place I know on the edge of a field that's like the local lovers lane. Although I had frequented it at one time, it was many, many years ago. (I had heard a rumour recently that it was now used as a 'dogging' site.) We park up and the kissing and stroking resumes.

Sex and the Signposts
Gaynor Evans

He is quick to begin an assault on my thighs and the moment his hands reach my knickers and he slips his fingers inside me, I know I am at the place of no return. Throwing my head back as his fingers force their way in, I am completely at his mercy. My car is a convertible, so it's not easy to manoeuvre in. Steve tries to undo his trousers, whilst still facing me, and is forced into the foot well on the passenger side. He is still inside me with one hand and trying to undo his trousers with the other. The gear stick is in the way and I glance at the back seat to see whether it offers any more room. Deciding that the answer is 'no' I'm trying to think of a solution; my blood was up (and no! I don't mean a hot flush) and I am determined to have him. Steve is all fingers and thumbs and lunges to kiss me again, trying to keep the momentum going. He is extremely excited and says breathlessly "I want you so much." At this point, having struggled with his belt and zip, he manages to set his penis free.

Because of his petite build, I was curious to know what was on offer in the Willy department. As he takes it out and plays with it in full view of me I am pleasantly surprised. It is a good size and rather beautiful. Now I definitely want it, but the question is how? Deciding that the only way is going to have be on his lap, I get him to sit down and I clamber over the gear stick and somehow manage to get my knees on each side of him. With my head hitting the roof, I manage to lower myself down on his cock. It's not comfortable but it's exciting. I

Sex and the Signposts
Gaynor Evans

help him to undo my buttons and he lifts one breast out and then two and starts stroking and sucking my nipples with great tenderness. I move slowly up and down. It feels so good that I am able to ignore the fact that my head is hitting the roof repeatedly.

He comes very quickly, but staying where I was and kissing him some more and letting him play with my breasts and sticking them in his face, I find that once again he is hard. So we have an encore, delicious! This is what I love about 'toyboys', repeat performances are a regular occurrence. Thinking to myself that it's a good job he is pocket size this wouldn't have worked with a big guy, I reluctantly drive him back to the station.

Anyway - back to the sofa in hand. So repeating the scene from the car I sit him down and straddle him, sliding down onto his hard and beautiful cock. Covering his pretty face in kisses, I ride him slowly. God I love this position! Steve tries to rev up the pace, like most 'toyboys' he likes to go at it like a steam train. I like it slow and work up to a crescendo, having savoured the first thrust or two. He whispers in my ear the word 'doggie'. I happily slide off and assume the position resting my head and arms on the sofa. He enters me and he is now totally in control and is taking me fast and at full pelt. I love being in charge, but I also love being submissive and let him loose to go about his business.

Sex and the Signposts
Gaynor Evans

This position, as any woman knows, is always very intense and has a number of distinct advantages. It makes for a tighter fit; it gets in really deep and frankly can be almost painful, but not quite. The pleasure is off the Richter scale. He manages to keep going and going and then giving me the usual announcement, he comes with permission.

I realise at this point just how drunk I am, and suggest that we go to bed. He follows me up the stairs and we hop into bed. Cuddling up, we fall asleep instantly, but it's not long before I'm wide awake. I never sleep well with a boy in my bed; my ex-husband having done such a good job of convincing me that I snore so loudly I could wake the dead. So I lay on the surface of sleep keeping myself in check. I open my eyes and look across at Steve, who is sleeping like a baby. He has such an angelic face and I keep my eyes open for some time, admiring my prize and feeling rather smug. At some point in the night, we cuddle up and get tangled up in the sheets together. It's nice having a cuddle, something I do miss from being in a regular relationship. That special person that is there just for you, when being held is the only thing that will help. Ah! Well mustn't dwell on what I'm missing, just enjoy what I'm having instead.

Morning breaks and I am hoping for some more action before work. We start kissing and he becomes erect and hard within seconds and I move down kissing every inch of his firm body on the

Sex and the Signposts
Gaynor Evans

way, then taking his cock in my mouth, I suck, lick and tease. I sense that he is very excited and loving my work, is already on the brink. Not wanting an early breakfast, I move back up and he quickly enters me. It's all over in a matter of seconds and he apologises immediately, saying that he was so aroused by my blow job he couldn't contain himself. Oh well, nice to know I'm good at BJ's I suppose, but I really would have liked a proper seeing to!

As we had no more time he goes off for a shower and comes back into the room in just a towel, which he drops to the floor. I'm still draped over the bed in a languid mood and find myself admiring his body once again. Perfectly flat stomach, lean and hard, every muscle is defined and he has a lovely cheeky backside. He really is rather beautiful and I wish we had time to go back to bed. God! I was almost salivating. We make small talk over tea and toast and I drop him back at the station with a sigh!

I'm at my desk by nine o'clock and spend five minutes giving Chloe a blow by blow account of my night, no pun intended! It had been a lovely evening and later in the week I had my gorgeous young Irishman to look forward to.

Sex and the Signposts
Gaynor Evans

Chapter Sixteen
DANNY BOY

He arrives at the station, a little late as usual. I watch him lumbering up the road in his very distinctive way and it never fails to amaze me that such an ungraceful man child can be such an artist in the bedroom.

He has a lovely face, strong chin and a penetrating gaze from his deep set dark green eyes. He kisses me briefly and we set off, chatting away, as it is some weeks since I have seen him. I groan inwardly to myself thinking he still looks twelve and I am a very bad woman.

Once at the flat, we have a drink and some pasta that I prepare very quickly in the kitchen. He follows me from room to room restlessly, until being unable to contain himself anymore he grabs me and kisses me passionately. He has the most kissable lips and I am aroused immediately.

Eating dinner unceremoniously on the sofa, we chat about this and that but the tension is building and the moment the plates go down he is upon me telling me I'm looking well, gorgeous, and sexy. His soft Irish accent lends itself well to pillow talk and I find its undulating rhythm almost hypnotic.

He starts pulling at my clothes and me at his. He removes his shirt, I take off my cardi. He is frantic,

Sex and the Signposts
Gaynor Evans

kissing me long and hard and I feel his desire and mine rise. Unable to bear it any longer, I pull the remainder of my clothes over my head and taking off my jeans and knickers with one hand, I use the other to push him back onto the sofa amongst the cushions. He is sitting down and I am climbing on, lowering myself down slowly onto his very hard cock.

I ride him gently and with every movement he thrusts upward to meet me. Losing ourselves in the moment, the age gap has become irrelevant. My hormones being an equal match for his, we hold each other's gaze and our enjoyment of each other is clearly visible on our faces, making the whole experience more intense. We get up and quickly go into the bedroom and resume our play.

He has the ability to take me to a place that I have never been before, and I am in such a state of arousal that I can't come back and it last for hours, as does his ability to go on and on. The kissing, the licking, the stroking, and the sucking, never stops. Our basic animal instincts have taken over and it feels truly amazing. So we go on. He says my name softly, over and over in his Irish way and the large gold cross that he always wears drops on my face, reminding me that he is a good catholic boy. Despite my efforts to repel it the thought pops into my head "I wonder what his mother would say?" My slight pang of guilt is eroded away by kisses to

Sex and the Signposts
Gaynor Evans

my neck and breasts, and I am drawn back in and can only feel and not think.

He rises and falls quickly, taking me further and further to that place of no return and then moaning softly he explodes inside me. Holding me tightly, and kissing me all over my face, he is still and we lay there quietly with just the noise of our laboured breathing filling the room.

A few moments pass and he begins to kiss me again on my face, and then my neck, working slowly down, taking my nipples in his mouth one at a time. Then moving on to my stomach, soft gentle kisses as he wriggles down adjusting my thighs en route, so he is in position. I am in such a state of arousal and the anticipation of what is to come is almost unbearable. Lifting my arms above my head, I offer myself up to him as he kisses each thigh slowly, drawing out the moment when his tongue meets my inner place.

He probes and licks searching, searching, until he is there, using the sound of my moans to navigate. It takes a few seconds to bring me to the brink. He remains still and quiet and doesn't move an inch. Suddenly there it is. The waves start growing from somewhere in the pit of my stomach, taking me up higher and higher. My moaning gets louder and sharper and suddenly I am released in an explosion of sensory messages that cause me to arch my back so violently that I have to hold his head in my hands

Sex and the Signposts
Gaynor Evans

to stop him losing his place and I am done, spent, and exhausted, but with the biggest smile on my face. I look at him as he climbs back up my body and I say to him "Thanks! You are clever." He smiles, kisses me again and we curl up, cosy and warm. "Are you happy?" he asks "very", I answer. "Me too" he says, and we promptly fall asleep.

Sex and the Signposts
Gaynor Evans

Chapter Seventeen
FRUSTRATIONS AND ERUPTIONS

Writing in my diary as usual I stare at the date and think why it is so significant? The 16th April must hold some meaning, but it takes me a while in my misty morning brain to remember. And then I have it! Had he been alive my horse Guinness would have been mine for Twenty seven years today. He had been with me at the end of my last marriage and had seen me in and out of my last one. My relationship with this handsome male had been devoted and loyal and he had given me great comfort throughout my troubles. When overwhelmed by life, I would go and sit quietly in the back of his stable whilst he munched on some hay. I would throw my arms around him and sob into his neck and although disturbed by the noise he would stand still and let me do it. It was a sad day last July then, when just too old and too tired to carry on he lay down in his stable and then just couldn't get up.

My daughters and I made the decision that he had had enough and with the vet in agreement he was put down. I would always be grateful for my time with this magnificent animal he had been a great friend and companion and lots of fun. Maybe both my husband's always felt they came rather low in the pecking order behind him and the children. I had often thought this was one of the reasons my relationships broke down but at least unlike my

Sex and the Signposts
Gaynor Evans

husband's he was loyal faithful and true.

I always feel that April is the month for looking forward and making changes and I had made many big decisions in this month in previous years; Buying the aforementioned animal, leaving my first husband, moving house, the death of my dad, the birth of my daughter. So in my book April is the month for reflection. Winter is over, well usually, but the winter of 2010 had been a hard one to bear. Everything and I mean everything, had been hard. It had been the longest coldest and gloomiest winter we had had in many a year and I've seen a few. There was endless snow causing havoc everywhere, swine flu causing illness everywhere and the worst and most protracted recession for over fifty years.

I am feeling more anxious than usual and my mood for the last few weeks has been a notch or two lower then my normal positive glass half full one, despite summer stretching tantalizing before me with all its heady delights to look forward to. Ascot, Wimbledon a week in Puerto Banus. Not to mention the promise of those long languid summer evenings. I just cannot shake off the feeling of apprehension and have spent the last two weeks second guessing myself and questioning my behaviour. I mean what am I doing with my life?

The absence of a toyboy fix despite opportunities being available my end as my son has been away, has knocked my confidence. The house empty for a

Sex and the Signposts
Gaynor Evans

week and I couldn't get one! Not one, of my favourite toyboys to come and play and even new dates have been so lean on the ground, that I have been blown out more times than a windsock. Couple that with the fact that my previous knee trouble seems to be back with a vengeance and I find myself feeling, dare I say it rather old. God! Did I actually write that? The last couple of weeks have been a damp squib. I have been drinking too much and getting bad tempered and I know that I am not in a good place. I need to realign my Karma.

Family worries are eating away at my well being. My mum who is 89 is getting frailer and has had to have some tests recently, although she is still feisty and certainly has all her marbles. I only hope I have inherited some of her genes. My eldest son is about to become a father and although this is a good and joyous occasion I am just not sure he is ready. He is a complicated boy and I'm afraid my lack of supplying him with a really good role model has taken its toll. On the work front the slog continues, recruitment is not the place to be during a recession and I drag myself in day after day and it's an uphill battle. I've been doing the same thing for the last twenty five years. God help me!

Talking of God it would seem that even he and the universe are conspiring against me and the very thing that will lift my spirits. My favourite toyboy, the one that brings me joy on all levels went home to Ireland for the Easter holidays. The fact that this

Sex and the Signposts
Gaynor Evans

coincided with me having the house to myself was bad enough, the fact that he was going to be away for three weeks and had been too busy with Uni work to come visit me in the weeks before was highly frustrating. So just when his period of absence was due to conclude and I can almost feel his hands upon me a Volcano erupts in bloody Iceland! Now, you may think that I have gone raving mad and what possible bearing can that have on me getting laid. Let me explain.

The volcanic cloud of ash and dust that has been spewed into the atmosphere has drifted and settled over British air space. Never before have the airports been so paralysed. No planes and I mean none are flying and the skies are empty; Fears that the dust and ash will clog plane engines and cause them to stall has meant that nothing is allowed to take off or land. This has now gone on for five days and shows no sign of abating as eruptions keep happening. Insignificant as I am in the grand scheme of things the result of this is that my "little one" can't get back to Blighty at the moment. The ferries are chock-a-block and the situation is set to continue. Short of stripping off and swimming the channel he is there and I am here. A swim in ice-cold water is actually not a bad idea from my point of view as I am exceptionally horny and no amount of self help is relieving the situation. So "Thank you God!!"

Sex and the Signposts
Gaynor Evans

Chapter Eighteen
FITNESS FIRST

Yesterday had been the much anticipated and long time coming evening, with the delightful 'Personal Trainer' that I had met on TBW (the website for the older woman and younger man scenario). We have been chatting for months via email, text and phone calls. Bright, fun, and always full of sensible down to earth advice, he would text or phone me out of the blue, but always seemed to wriggle out of any arrangements to meet. He seems to want to be impulsive and meet on the spur of the moment, which is hard for me, given my domestic work and family commitments. I find him very entertaining, and on the sexual front, he only occasionally digresses into naughty texts, and then apologises for it! Although I did watch him being very naughty on webcam once, and wasn't put off - in fact, I liked it - which is unusual for me, as I don't like the voyeuristic side to the internet, I'd rather be involved!

Months have passed, but he keeps in the loop and I have long since given up any hope of getting my hands on his fitness instructor body. Then, one Monday morning, after my repeated requests to give me more notice, I get a text asking what my plans are for the week. I list my itinerary - a funeral today, night out in the City on Thursday, but nothing, other than that. An hour elapses, and at this stage I should point out that men and 'toyboys'

Sex and the Signposts
Gaynor Evans

in particular are terrible texters. They don't reply for hours, days, weeks, and then act as if the text you sent had just arrived. They never get to the point and rarely ring if a text would do. The only exception is when they are trying to win you over, or are horny and want to talk dirty. Then, you get an immediate reply and you can virtually feel the heat. A prime time for this is late Saturday and Sunday mornings; when they are hung over, horny and still in bed, or last thing, late into the night when they are drink fuelled. Anyway, back to the story. My phone rings and he asks me cheerfully what I'm doing Tuesday evening. I reply nothing and he says shall we do something? "Yes please, anything would be nice" is my immediate answer, so we arrange to meet in Camden Town where he is flat sitting for a relative. Experience tells me to take nothing for granted as another downside to toyboys is their ability to get distracted and forget arrangements.

Tuesday comes and although I am hoping our date is still on, I am fully expecting to be blown out. I live in a perpetual state of anxiety when dates have been arranged. Will he? Won't he? I text him in the afternoon "just checking to see if we are still on for later ? " he texts back "Yep absolutely". Wow, I am impressed, but still not convinced. He has given me very specific driving instructions and assures me it isn't far.

Anyone who knows me well knows that my driving

Sex and the Signposts
Gaynor Evans

ability is limited to short distances on local terrain. I had only been driving a few years and had always been terribly nervous. My husband's used to drive me everywhere but the need to drive became more essential as my marriage hit the skids and the kids moved out, so like a lot of things, I was a late starter and venturing out of my comfort zone, and near to London, is enough to make me over anxious. We arrange for me to arrive at about 6.30pm, straight from work. Despite his instructions, I decide to check on route finder and I am horrified to find that it is much further than I thought and I start to have a real wobble. Unknown busy roads in the rush hour, crossing the North Circular and to make it worse, it's dark and raining, so I ring him and tell him how worried I am, and he assures me that its one straight road.

Pulling myself together and giving myself a good talking to, I re-apply my makeup, change tights for stockings and set off. He rings me constantly en route, to check my progress, which I find both endearing and annoying at the same time as I don't answer the phone when I'm driving and don't have "hands free". My journey is not without event and I get lost, twice, finally pulling over near a sign that says 'Central London' this way. Oh my god!! Now what? I phone him and he tells me I have gone too far turn and to turn round and come back. Everything is one way and I am having a panic attack. I drive back and find a side road and call him again. Asking me what I can see he gets an

Sex and the Signposts
Gaynor Evans

idea of where I am and sets of on foot, in the rain, to find me.

I sit in the car getting more and more nervous. We have exchanged pictures and I have seen him on web cam but he hasn't seen me. It's more important that he likes me than I like him. Don't ask me why, a confidence thing I suppose, but always the same. My door opens and there he is. Wet from the rain and grinning. I quickly assimilate what he looks like and I can see that resistance will be futile! He has broad well defined shoulders and is tall and lean and hiding what looks like a well built body. He has a mop of jet black hair, much longer than in his pictures, and a big plus for me as I love, love, love, long hair. He has large brown eyes and a nice soft voice. Ok, I'm in. He kisses me on the cheek and asks what I'd like to do? Go for a drink or straight back to the flat? Looking at the weather I give the flat my vote and I'm not worried, I feel I know him quite well after months of dialogue have reassured me. He jumps out to get some wine and I watch him walking away, and back, admiring his upright stance and the way he moves.

He directs me to the flat, which is in a large regency building with massive steps. We go up to the second floor and he leads me in and we settle down on the sofa, wine in hand. I feel relaxed and comfortable. He makes no overtly sexual advances, his body language is contained, and we chatter

Sex and the Signposts
Gaynor Evans

happily about his business and mine. I am enjoying the wine (he chose a nice bottle) and then suddenly during our conversation our eyes meet and my stomach lurches into my throat. The chemistry is strong. We both feel it, but look back at our drinks, and the conversation continues. A little later our eyes meet again and this time we hold each other's gaze 'God, he is yummy!' Breaking the spell, he leans in and says "I'm gonna be cheeky and plant one on you." I don't move, indicating that 'planting one on me' is more than acceptable. Our lips meet, then our tongues and my stomach leaves the room via the roof. I am lost in the moment but I know that if I pull back he will be happy to withdraw. There is something of the gentleman about this guy.

We pull apart and sit holding hands for a while. Then unable not to, we resume the kissing which becomes more frantic and his hand slides up my skirt and inside my knickers. I am wet with excitement and gasp as his fingers slide easily inside me. I go from nought to a hundred very quickly and in my head I thank God for HRT. He stops taking off his top and I'm left admiring the naked broad shoulders, the arms, the pecks, all gorgeous! He has a large 'Robbie Williams' type tattoo around one of his biceps. I'm not a fan of tattoos but it looks 'right' on him. He reaches down and undoes his trousers, releasing his cock into the wild. I play with it and know without a doubt that there will be no stopping now. I am going to have to have this sexy dark-haired young man. I produce a condom, as if by magic, and without complaint he slides it on easily. I stand and hop out of my knickers and kneeling astride him I lower myself down onto his lap and slowly, slowly, inch by inch, savouring every single centimetre, I take him inside me. God! I love this bit and I really am getting obsessed with this position.

Kissing him softly and running my fingers through his jet black hair, I rise and fall gently. He kisses my breasts and holds me tightly. It is an exquisite ride. I have a feeling it's not going to be a marathon but it doesn't need to be. We are lost for that moment, connecting as only a male and female can. The age gap melts away at this point. He comes fairly quickly and apologises, blaming my sexiness. But I am content. When it scores this high, ten minutes is more memorable than a long drawn out pounding that doesn't even engage all the senses. We cuddle up and then get dressed; he puts just his jeans on and goes into the kitchen and I have full view of his toned torso, his long black hair in a state of disarray, flopping over his eyes. An example of a man at his best, I think to myself and 'Gaynor you're a lucky woman'.

He makes me coffee and toast and cuddles up to me whilst I eat. Sometime later, I have to leave as he has early morning clients and I also have work. He is protective and caring about my journey home and escorts me part of the way to ensure I don't get lost, and is happy to walk back in the rain. I manage to

Sex and the Signposts
Gaynor Evans

get home without too much trouble and have time to wonder at myself and what I get up to. If I never see him again, it was unforgettable. He phones me to make sure I got home safely and seems keen on seeing me again. I, for my part, would love another encounter.

NB: It has been some months since I have seen him and although we are still in touch, we have yet to revisit the scene, but I live in hope!

Sex and the Signposts
Gaynor Evans

Chapter Nineteen
PATIENCE IS A VIRTUE

If there is one skill that I have acquired in bucket loads during my dalliances with Toyboys it is patience. Frankly you need to have it in abundance if you are to going to survive dating the younger male. The amount of times they turn up late or even worse get sidetracked and have to rearrange is in endless supply.

My favourite Danny is a prime example. We had made an arrangement to meet one evening as usual, my friends empty flat was available so an opportunity not to be missed. He was aiming to get to me at 7pm and I knew this meant nearer 8pm and to be fair he does have three train changes to make and it is an arduous journey. Then I get a text at 5pm to say he was running late and it would be nearer 9pm and "was that ok?" I always feel like answering well the sooner the better but I nod inwardly to myself and reply "that's fine Hun" Can't be giving young students too much pressure. I text him again to check that nine means nine having spent some time making myself as desirable as possible and packing supplies for our night together Pizza, sweets sausages for breakfast and some booze of course.

The reply wings back "nearer ten by my reckoning" followed by "do you still want me to come?" **Do I still want him to come?!!** Is he raving mad?

Sex and the Signposts
Gaynor Evans

Having worked myself up into a frenzy of anticipation and as always being sexually charged and emotionally in need of a fix, the mere fact he can even consider not coming sends me into a complete panic. Taking a very deep breathe I answer matter-of-factly "of course". He answers with "see you soon then". Growling to myself I stifle my irritation that I now have two hours to kill (Of course he will spend most of that time travelling across London) I drive to my friends flat where our rendezvous will take place. (This is the aforementioned flat of my good friend Amanda whose mum has Alzheimer's) Amanda is away for two weeks and I am in charge of cat and flat.

Her poor mum is now happily settled in a suitable home and all that remains of the 'signs' is the mark where the Blue-Tac used to be that held them up. Amanda had text me earlier in the day to see if I had made good use of her facilities and I had told her "no, not yet" Unfortunately her holiday had coincided with my daughters holiday to Spain with her girlfriend (she needed a break) and I had been in charge of Matilda for a six day period and this had not allowed me to 'play Cougar'. I found this very frustrating with the flat available for so long. Amanda's reply was "Well hurry up". I laughed she does like to think of me putting her bed to good use when she is away. No pressure then and I replied that tonight was the night!!

Sex and the Signposts
Gaynor Evans

I get cosy on the sofa watching Tuesday night TV which actually isn't bad 'Holby' at 8pm followed by 'Vampire Diaries' at 9pm two of my favourites. Before I know it the time flies by and it's approaching 9.45pm. I jump in the car and drive up to Oakwood station a journey I have made many times. I park in the slip road opposite, it's quite dark now and I lock my doors having been accosted here once before by a young man wanting my phone number and to join me in the car. It's now 10pm and I wait patiently. Its fifteen minutes before I see his distinctive figure coming towards me in the dark. He climbs in and kisses me and I inwardly let out a sigh of relief.

I drive quickly in the direction of the flat whilst he chats to me. He is very animated and excited and tells me all about the film he has just made and sites this as the reason he is late.

Once inside we relax chatting for ages, catching up. I have booked the next day off work so I don't have to rush him off in the morning and so I can spend more time with my 'little one'. I know from experience that I will probably be far too tired to function anyway.

We manage to keep our hands off each other for a whole hour and then our hands touch and we start stroking each other's fingers, turning them this way and that. I raise his hand to my mouth and suck his fingers gently. This very erotic gesture sends me

Sex and the Signposts
Gaynor Evans

into a stomach churning flurry of anticipation and our eyes meet. More stomach lurching is followed by soft sensual kissing as we start unbuttoning, unzipping and pulling at our clothes. Finally as our tongues slide into each other's mouths we are naked and I straddle him pushing him back on the sofa lowering myself down and taking him inside me. I moan loudly. This is without doubt my favourite part-the moment of entry. He knows this and allows me to go slow, slow, slowly even though he wants to go fast, fast, faster! This blissful lovemaking goes on for quite some time until it's almost too much to bear. I watch his face change as he comes deep inside me and we sit for a while holding each other and kissing a lot, with him still firmly in my grip. Frankly, I hate taking him out but having had my knees folded under my weight for a while I realise that I am in pain and need to stretch it out (Oh the joys of getting older!) I carefully extricate myself from his lap and we sit naked under a blanket, recovering quietly.

A film comes on the TV which he tell me is a good one and for a while we sit side by side holding hands and watching it in complete contented silence. Deciding to put the pizza in the oven as I haven't eaten yet I stand up managing to get in his way at a crucial moment in the film. Apologising I say "sorry I spoilt your view" without hesitation and looking me straight in the eyes he says "You are the view". I burst out laughing and slapping him hard I say "you charmer" but loving the comment all the

Sex and the Signposts
Gaynor Evans

same. After the pizza and the film we creep into the bedroom.

The rest of the night, what's left of it is spent in a sexual frenzy with not one, not two but three delicious orgasms for me teased out by his capable tongue, and just when we thought we'd had enough, I begin playing with his balls and stoking him very gently. This has the most amazing effect on his flaccid and worn out penis. It rises skyward and inflates to three times its size and groaning he pushes me down and enters me for the umpteenth time. "Oh my god I am insatiable" I think to myself and then realize that I have said it out loud. He looks down at me and says "does that mean I'm rubbish?" "Far from it" I reply "I just can't get enough of you". He smiles and the kissing resumes along with the lovemaking. I realise that we are swiftly running out of time. My phone keeps going off, work, my friend, and my other Irish toy boy keen to tell me all about a dream he has just had about me. Oops!

We get up and dress and I make sausage sandwiches and coffee which he really appreciates. We had worked up quite an appetite. It's not long now before I will be driving back to Oakwood station. Reluctantly he gathers up his stuff and follows me out to the car. I decide to come back and tidy the flat later. We climb in the car and I say brightly "Roof down"? He nods and my car does its transformer thing and he says "could we go for a

Sex and the Signposts
Gaynor Evans

drive" I say "yes of course if you want to?" I would love to hang onto him for a bit longer. But I remember he has an essay to write and a deadline to meet and I say "look at the time". He pulls a face and says "better go back to the station" I know that his work is important to him.

He is always very quiet on the journey back to the station he listens to my CD and stares out of the window. We park in the same place, where I had waited patiently the night before. We look at each other and kiss over and over again. I grab his hand and he grabs mine back. With the roof down I feel rather exposed and as an old lady passes by on the pavement. I giggle and mumble something about being seen kissing a boy in public. He doesn't seemed bothered and we kiss some more. He says softly but with conviction "I will see you soon" I nod and he says "Well I had better go, before we go back to the flat" and reluctantly dragging his feet he gets out of the car. "Or before I don't let you go at all" I quip back, forcing a smile that I'm not really feeling. He walks away and looks back at me over his shoulder and grins broadly.

I drive by slowly and he keeps his gaze firmly on me. I take this as a sign that he doesn't really want to go and it is of some comfort. But I know from experience that the sinking feeling will soon return once the endorphins begin to wane and before long I will be looking for my next 'fix' but for the moment I feel boosted satiated and so tired I could

Sex and the Signposts
Gaynor Evans

sleep on a washing line. I am definitely sporting that 'I've just been shagged senseless look' glazed eyes and dilated pupils and although I have tried to flatten it I have the usual 'sex hair' that comes from spending far too long in the missionary position.

I park up outside my Victorian terrace and walking slowly inside I draw the blinds and crawl onto the sofa for nap. I am going out to dinner with my best friend Trudy tonight where tales of my night's antics will be the topic of the evening's conversation and a fitting end to my day.

I stay in an up-beat mood for the next few days and send my 'little one' a text which is usual for me "that he was amazing and that I hope he got his essay in on time followed by a 'Mwaah"! I don't expect a reply for some time which is the usual for him and as I said earlier you need an abundance of patience. After a few days have passed my feelings of elation sink like a stone. I get a text from him about four days later saying that he had a great time and would see me soon.

This was not to be for some three weeks, his Uni work must take precedence. In the meantime I am getting texts from other Toyboys including my sexy Aussie who seems to be warming up nicely after a period of absence. The Aussie will have a hard act to follow but I'm willing to let him try. He will be a distraction from my growing attachment to my young Irishman. I go to bed that night reciting to

Sex and the Signposts
Gaynor Evans

myself "must not get too attached" "must not get too attached".

My form of self-hypnosis is set to fail miserably. After the next particularly joy filled meeting with Danny I find myself getting more and more anxious. It's been two weeks since I have seen him and although I had told him that I didn't know when he could come again because of lack of opportunity at my end, we had agreed to speak. I had text him over the weekend in a moment of weakness, bought on by six gin and tonics and half a bottle of wine. They really should invent some sort of cure for this behaviour. I know from speaking to my girlfriends that the drunken late night text mistake is commonplace. You feel full of confidence and the object of your desire becomes a focus and you think bravely that you have something really important to tell them. You ignore that fact that its 3am in the morning and texting might not be a good idea.

I remember one night when I was under strict instructions from my daughter that on no account was I to allow her to text a certain person at the end of the evening when she was feeling the full force of her vodka and tonics. When the moment came and she had her phone poised ready, I had to chase her around the kitchen prising it out of her hands and hiding it quickly, ignoring her loud drunken protests. She was however very grateful in the morning when her head had cleared. I'm sure most of the girls out there know that sinking feeling, you

Sex and the Signposts
Gaynor Evans

open your eyes and feeling bleary eyed and extremely hungover, you have this vague recollection of texting person or persons unknown. Reaching for your phone, which is usually sleeping in the bed with you, you check the sent box. Screaming inwardly you realize that you have done it again!!! You have text Joe or Steve or Dan even though you had left strict instructions with yourself that you were never to text them again. Well it's too late now.

So my late night drunken text had hit Danny's inbox and unusually I had got an immediate response. We had a light hearted dialogue finishing on speak soon xx. Now soon is a strange word and can be hopelessly misinterpreted. 'Soon' to me is within the next 48 hours but to a man\boy in his twenties it is sometime in the distance future. Because after all he has all the time in the world, unlike you! So by Thursday I had decided that 'soon' had arrived so I send him a text. This would be my feeble attempt at trying to getting control of the situation.

The weekend passes and I still haven't had a reply. By Tuesday I am ridiculously anxious and even a long text session from my sexy Aussie does not soothe me. With my imagination working overtime I tell myself that he has had enough of travelling to see me and that he is never coming again and I am really upset at the thought of it. Reading this back to myself I know that it is ridiculous, laughable and

Sex and the Signposts
Gaynor Evans

obscene almost. I mean what am I thinking? This is a fledgling man-child I am dealing with, virtually a spotty adolescent. But he has touched and moved me in a way that I didn't think possible in one so young. He has met me on many levels mentally as well as physically. The sex is amazing and the conversation entertaining so why no contact? It's not unusual for weeks to pass before I hear from him but somehow this feels different. I am experiencing a strong sense of loss and I am really missing his physical presence.

I realize that I am not in a good place here and I need to get a grip!! He has got under my skin with his gentle ways, foot massages, wine and chocolates stimulating conversation, not to mention the multiple orgasms. I hope that he has just lost his phone or been too busy with Uni work to fit me in and the urge to text him again rises to the surface but I know I mustn't. The only way this situation could be worse than it is already is if I send another text and that gets ignored as well. I mean how long does it take to send a reply? I give myself a good talking too but I know that despite my best efforts I have allowed this young man to figure too highly in the scheme of things. I have broken my own rules but sometimes, just sometimes I have to let my heart rule my head.

Fifteen minutes after all this angst I receive a text from him followed by a long phone call. I am ridiculously happy and as sure as eggs is eggs, heading for heartache. But does that stop me? What do you think?

NB Danny and I continue our passion for each other during the coming summer months until he has to return home at the end July 2010 with promises of revisiting the scene when he comes back in the autumn. Despite keeping in touch the months go by and he doesn't materialise. I eventually come to the conclusion that he has moved on and I just have to deal with it.

Sex and the Signposts
Gaynor Evans

Chapter Twenty
BABES IN BANUS

July 2010 was to be the month for my second 'girls on Tour holiday'. I had joined my daughter and two friends last year for a five day trip to Puerto Banus Spain in May 2009. I loved the port and had come a few times with my Ex-husband doing the 'couple 'thing. Beach days and nice romantic dinners in the evening, this was a **completely** different experience. I was initiated into the whole idea of partying till dawn, with strict instructions from my daughter to just go with the flow and do as they do. I was determined to embrace my new found freedom so I did as I was told and we had a wild time. So I was really looking forward to chapter two, having loved my first hedonistic experience. It was unusual for me to have no one to consider but myself and it felt very liberating.

Last year's apartment was in the heart of the port and had all the amenities close by. This included the local supermarket for the booze and food, the beach for the sunbathing and the clubs and bar for the pulling and fun! The port also boasted a brilliant shopping plaza with all the best and poshest shops if only we had the money. So with no cabs involved we could walk or stagger to and from the apartment. Last year had been a steep learning curve for me. It seems you have to turn your body clock on its head and sleep during the day and party all night. I soon got the hang of it and was often the last girl

Sex and the Signposts
Gaynor Evans

standing. Stamina and me, it would appear are old friends. Well that or the miracles of HRT and my newly found libido. On my first trip I had managed to find a lot of very desirable young men. My pulling power amazed me! I attracted all sorts and had given the benefit of my womanly charms to just two lucky recipients. The first one was kind enough to escort me back to my apartment when I was hopelessly lost. It was 4 am in the morning and I had been chatting to him inside when I realised I had lost everyone and had no idea how to navigate back to the apartment.

He was English born but a native as he lived and worked in Spain. With his help I managed to get back to the apartment without him I would have been hopelessly lost. The others were all ensconced inside as came through the door, except for Olivia who had gone AWOL with young guy she had met earlier. My escort and I and I'm sorry, but I still to this day cannot remember his name, wandered into the apartment and greeted the others. They were just glad to see me and he did seem very likeable and was polite and friendly to everyone. .He was sporting a few stitches to his left eye which I did quiz him about and apparently he had got into a fight a few days before. This didn't faze me at all, as far as I was concerned he had been the perfect gentleman.

Eventually we retired to the bedroom and although very drunk I remember the whole thing quite

Sex and the Signposts
Gaynor Evans

vividly (all except his name of course)…he helped me out of my clothes until I was standing there in just my underwear. He kissed me all over before taking my Bra firmly in one hand he tore it from my body, Grrr very caveman! Lots of extremely hot sex followed and I even had the foresight to produce condoms judging by the amount (used) that were strewn on the floor it seems we had got through quite a few.

I awoke in the morning having passed out with no recollection of him going, but gone he was. I realised that he could easily have ransacked the flat, on his way out and bleary-eyed, I raised myself onto my elbows and surveyed the scene…clothes everywhere and a torn and broken bra draped over the end of the bed. I reached for my bag to check. No everything was still there money included and sitting next to me was a full glass of water, something I would never have got for myself and another sign that he really had been a nice guy. I did discover something was missing after further investigation. He had gone to the kitchen and helped himself to the leftover pasta that was sitting on top of the microwave and frankly he was more than welcome. I never saw him again.

It was on our last evening out, that my friend pulled a gorgeous young man and I ended up with his friend by default, very pretty and amazingly good in bed and an embryo! When the sun rose they panicked, realising they where well out of their

Sex and the Signposts
Gaynor Evans

depth and did a runner, leaving us laughing at their terror. We must have looked **very** scary in the morning; All in all I had really enjoyed my first ever girls holiday abroad. In my youth a trip to Butlin's was all one could hope for!! Well that or a day trip to Southend and a bag of fish and chips.

So when it came to booking for 2010 I was excited and really looking forward to it. Unfortunately the apartment we had rented last year had been sold and we had a real; problem finding one so centrally placed. But eventually my daughter found a likely contender, that looked lovely but we were really worried about the location. We looked it up on the maps and the owners reassured us that it wasn't far away from the port and within walking distance, ten minutes tops from the beach we loved and the clubs and bars that we favoured, 'Sinatra's' and 'Linekers'. We had some serious reservations about the exact location but having come up with nothing nearer we booked it. Fly out on the 8th July and come back on the 15th sorted!

Two weeks before the holiday, the mad furore begins. What to take? Do we need new Bikinis? What factor? Wax or Shave? Phone calls fly back and forth followed by endless texts about shoes, hair straightner's, hair dryers and condoms!!! Finally with our bags packed, we creep out in the middle of the night to head for Luton Airport. I hate flying but I am getting better and managed to board the plane alcohol free. I did succumb to a couple of

Sex and the Signposts
Gaynor Evans

Gordon's and tonics once we were in the air just to settle me into the holiday mood. Although I knew my stomach was in for some serious drinking in the days ahead, warming it up seemed a good idea.

Our cab was waiting and we made the forty five minute journey from Malaga airport to our apartment. The cab driver a Brit was not that familiar with the location and it took a few attempts to find it. It was right next door to a posh newly vamped hotel call Sisu. Eventually we arrived and met the rep who was there to greet us. The apartment was very posh, three bedrooms two bathrooms lovely marble floors and a balcony overlooking the N340 road!! Oh well!

Our immediate question was "how far are we from our usual haunts?" We unpacked quickly and decided to explore but the initial signs were not good. We could see the two hotels that rise above the skyline in Banus itself. 'The PYR' and 'The Benabola' and were the landmark to head for, But they were a long way in the distance. We set off in their direction in our flip flops with our beach bags in hand. We had a large flyover to cross to get on the 'Banus side' There was a garage that sold lots of essentials and this was to prove useful in the days that followed. So off we went busy traffic streaming past, sun beating down. At least it was warm.

We carefully crossed every road (the Spanish drivers are pretty ruthless and don't always stop

Sex and the Signposts
Gaynor Evans

even if you are halfway across) the fact that you have to look in the opposite direction to what you do back home makes crossing the road a dangerous affair. I got caught out by crossing, having looked the wrong way and didn't see an oncoming car. The Spanish driver was hanging out of his window yelling loudly in my direction "You Stupido" at the top of his voice. I thought charming! "Welcome to Spain Gaynor" as I scuttled across to get out of his way. His insult of "Stupido" was to prove very true of me later in the week however!

Ten minutes later in the extreme heat we were still on the hoof. Fifteen minutes and it was looking more hopeful as the shops honed into view. So it was at least a twenty minute walk. The description of a few minute's walk as per the brochure was hopelessly inept and cross as we were it was too late to do anything about it and we would just have to make the best of it. It was strikingly obvious though, that walking all this way in the evenings in our carefully chosen and packed stilettos was not an option. Weaving our way through the shops; Prada, Louis Vuitton, Caroline Herrera, we made our way down to 'Levante Beach'. It is in a very pretty bay with the Victory statute in prime position overlooking all he surveys hands held high. The mountains are stretched out on the left and covered in a low lying mist. Too the right there is a manmade breakwater of huge stones and boulders shaped like thimbles that tumble out into the calm blue azure waters. These are a haven for teenage

Sex and the Signposts
Gaynor Evans

boys wanting to practice their diving skills and many can be seen leaping off into the sea.

The soft white sand is so hot, you cannot stand on it for any length of time in bare feet and we walk quickly down to the rows and rows of sun beds that stretch out along the shoreline, their bright blue umbrellas flapping and spinning in the offshore breeze and matching the colour of the sky. Not a single cloud is visible and with two bars offering lunches and ice cold San Miguel or Pina Coladas on either side, the place is almost perfect and my idea of heaven. We park on our selected beds and stripping off we race down to the sea, splashing each other and giggling loudly as we cool off. Let the holiday begin.

We spend the next three of four hours laughing, chatting and browning ourselves and drinking in the view and some ice cold beers. The only blot on the landscape is being constantly bothered by the 'looky, looky men' who go up and down the beach relentlessly in search of a sale.

Offering you anything from kaftans to handbags, sunglasses to fake watches, they are persistent to the point of getting on your nerves and I wish someone would suggest that they might like to take a dip in the sea themselves. Frankly if you get down wind the smell is bloody awful.

Sex and the Signposts
Gaynor Evans

As the sun lowers in the sky we decide to head back aware that we have rather a trek on our hands. We pack up our bags and wend our way slowly back across the beach discussing the fact that a cab will be required for our first big night out later.

Back in the apartment, we are all exhausted after our long walk and flopping in front of the very large flat screen TV we put the news on from back home. We are all keen to know the latest update on the hunt for Raoul Moat Britain's most wanted man. Moat had come out of prison and gone on a shooting spree killing one seriously injuring `two others. They have him cornered in a field and the drama continues. Gradually one by one we all drift off to our beds or stay slumped on the sofa taking a much needed power nap. We would need all the energy we could muster for our night out later.

Then as we all come round rubbing our eyes and scratching our heads the fun begins; the big preparation for the lively night ahead. The 'getting ready' wine opened, Showers and baths in rotation the slapping on of after- sun to preserve the growing tan, hair dryers on and straighteners at the ready. Clothes are put on and then promptly taken off again. Opinions required at every stage of the proceedings. Is my hair straight at the back...could you plait me a headband (Olivia's speciality).these shoes or my black ones, is my back fat tucked in. Make-up passes from room to room with much giggling and everyone is in high spirits, The TV

Sex and the Signposts
Gaynor Evans

goes off and the music goes on and the second bottle of wine is uncorked and filling our glasses we gather on out balcony. (With views of the N340) for a photo shoot that will inevitably end up all over Facebook.

I really enjoy this bit of female bonding and the ritualistic way we all help each other out with confidence building comments and advice. Frankly we all look fantastic, nothing like a bit of a tan to bring out the whites of the eyes and teeth and give us all a healthy glow. Of course we can't compete with the beautiful people of Puerto Banus, those that come out for the elitist clubs and waft up and down the strip in shoe string dresses and Louboutin shoes. Enviable thin with perfect hair and nails they, are usually the right side of thirty, stunning and displaying man-made cleavages. (My breasts just have to fend for themselves). Good job then that they won't be frequenting the same places as us but sticking to the posh bars and clubs that Costa da fortune to party in.

We on the other hand will be mixing with the Brits abroad in Sinatra's bar and Lineker's and anywhere else along the way. By the time we are ready it is nearly midnight and with the clip clopping of our stilettos on the marble floors, echoing around the apartment we descend the stairs (carefully) and out onto the street in the hope of finding a cab driver. Luckily one was passing and was kind enough to call us another. It is only a five minute ride in a cab

Sex and the Signposts
Gaynor Evans

before we know is we are out in the Port.

The Yachts that line up in unison along the quay are nothing short of magnificent. Some are so huge and splendid that they are worth a king's ransom and are probably owned by one! They are a tourist attraction in their own right. The other common sight driving slowly past all the bars are the fast cars the Ferraris, Lamborghinis, Porches and Aston Martins. Every boys dream car is there revving their engines and crawling up and down the strip showing off. The smell of petrol blends well with the mixture of aftershave and perfume that is so strong it blots out the smell of the sea. All in all it's very high octane, but a vital part of the atmosphere.

Squeezing in at the bar in 'Sinatra's' we order a round of drinks, it's not the cheapest place but the very generous amount of spirits that they put in makes up for the price. After three or four of this super strength firewater sloshing about in our stomachs and mixing with the 'getting ready' wine we are well on our way to a very jolly evening. We sit on the quay chatting to different groups of guys and then make our way to slowly up the lanes to Lineker's. We are pestered on the way by club and bar promoters trying to get us to have a drink in one of their venues and we take tickets thinking maybe later (But later never seems to come).

Lineker's is buzzing already, its loud, packed and rocking. The DJ knows just what to play to get the

Sex and the Signposts
Gaynor Evans

crowd on side and he has the place on fire. The barmaids are gorgeous and the barman are all fit. Spotting one really sexy beast from last year we mosey over for a chat. One round of Sambuca shots later and we are all singing and dancing, giving it large! Various men come and go during the night and a bit of impromptu snogging takes place. The cameras are in and out of the handbags recording every indiscretion and funny moment. These will be carefully scrutinized in the haze of our hangovers tomorrow. We have a great evening and in a flash the music has stopped and its 4am and we are pouring out onto the street. As we bundle out of the door a young man with blonde hair and blue eyes asks me if I have had a good evening, I instantly recognise the Irish accent, swooning and smiling broadly I reply drunkenly that I have had a great time and had he?

We chat as we a pushed along in the crowd and deciding he is very cute, when he moves in for a kiss I'm happy to oblige. As I draw breathe he say why don't you come with me and my brother we are going to a club. His brother appears from behind him grinning and I'm looking at the same blond hair and blue eyes. My God! was I seeing double and then the penny drops twins! Both smiling and talking at me at once they grab me round the waist and try and drag me off with them. I protest and extricating myself as we get outside I send them on their way, shaking my head and laughing.

Sex and the Signposts
Gaynor Evans

One of their crowd a girl grabs me by the arm as she is passing and says to me in a broad Irish accent "do you know how old they are?" bemused by the question I shake my head I was thinking twenty something, hard to tell in the dark street and the issue was further clouded by the Sambuca shots!! Pausing for effect she whispers in my ear the word SIXTEEN! Oh My God! How embarrassing, I had no idea!! Even I wouldn't stoop that low intentionally and I am mortified and find myself apologizing to her. She thinks it is very funny and comments that I'm old enough to be their mother. I remember thinking "yes, and some!"

My friends having overheard all this are laughing loudly at my expense. My usually tolerant daughter is horrified and reprimands me very thoroughly. It is now 4.30am and I decide that on that note the 'old bird' better go home before she disgraces herself any further. So Louise and I go off to find a taxi. The others had spotted the nice crowd of guys that we had been talking to early on in the evening. They were from London and on a boys golfing holiday. They were staying in the PYR Hotel and they join forces and all head back in that direction. I'd heard a lot about this hotel but had never ventured in. Apparently the rooms have loads of beds crammed in and look rather like dormitories. It is very popular with guys that golf! I was to find out for myself later in the week when I live up to my new name of 'Stupido'

Sex and the Signposts
Gaynor Evans

Chapter Twenty One
CINDERELLA AND THE NOT SO CHARMING PRINCE

The next few days are spent perfecting our tans and enjoying the sights and sounds of Puerto Banus and suddenly find ourselves on our final night. The enthusiasm is over-spilling as we throw ourselves into our last evening. All wearing colours that complement our now deep and glowing tans we head out.

As we stroll down to the harbour, I see a guy across the street that I recognise, he is with a big crowd, but I am sure that I have met him before. He is tall and has unusual swept back hair which is quite long and a very distinctive face. He reminds me of a noble Red Indian Warrior and I am racking my brain trying to remember where I had seen him before. Maybe I had chatted to him online but I was sure that I actually knew him. Unable to conjure up who he was or where I had met him, I carry on with our last lively night.

Dancing until we drop we say our last goodbyes to Lineker's and as we walk out on the street I walk straight into the mysterious "Running Bear". I decide that I really must know who he is and thinking that I rather fancy him and being completely inebriated I bowl over and interrupt his conversation. Slurring slightly I ask him "where do we know each other from?" He smiles at me and

Sex and the Signposts
Gaynor Evans

studying my face he says "We met at Ascot". Ah, well no wonder I had no real recollection I would have been in a similar state to the one I'm in now. We chat happily and I am feeling a strong attraction that seems to be mutual. He comes from the Surrey area and tells me that he is on a double stag party in charge of the entertainment. We are constantly interrupted by his mates asking where they are going next. They had planned to go to a club and Rob asks me and the girls to go with them. We decide that we can't really and saying our goodbyes he reluctantly leaves to go and sort out his friends. Shame, I thought he was the only one so far that I had fancied some fun with and although I had had other opportunities, I hadn't been inspired, so hadn't got passed the kissing stage. All in all we had all been very well behaved unlike the last time we were here.

We made our way up through the streets chatting madly when suddenly there he was before me again. Grabbing me by the hand he said that he had sent his friends on ahead and had come back to look for me. By now there was only Olivia and I left. Kate had gone off for some private time with a very nice Spanish guy she had met earlier. One of Rob's friends came back looking for the whip money which he handed over and then seeing Olivia he began chatting her up. Rob suggests that we went back to his hotel room which was just across the road looking up I realised that he was talking about the famous PYR.

Sex and the Signposts
Gaynor Evans

Ah! Well about time I got a look inside I had heard so much about it. Holding hands he lead me across the road and looking back I could see Olivia and his friend following. In we went and he led me upstairs and into the room. It was as I had been told, quite basic, with six beds crammed in every which way. We were still talking a lot and he asked me if I'd like a drink. He got me a coke and we sat on the bed, I realised that we now on our own and had no idea where Olivia and his friend had gone. Rob told me all about his family and his job and then the kissing started and I decided that I really fancied him. We were both pretty drunk and it wasn't long before the kissing turned into foreplay and I knew there was no turning back.

I had a nagging doubt in my mind about the door being open and stopped him and said so. He assured me it was locked and went outside and demonstrated the fact and then reassured I undid my shoes throwing them on the floor and pulling my tangerine dress over my head I jumped on the bed (his one of the six) and he undressed himself. He was broad and tanned and very drunk and I had my work cut out, but by now my ardour was up. I fumbled in my bag for a condom, drunk I may be but I was taking no chances. He put up little protest and having worked hard to get him 'Up' he slid the condom on and with him laying flat on the bed I got on top and with my hair falling in his face we moved in time and we were beginning to really connect.

Sex and the Signposts
Gaynor Evans

My phone alarm went off and then I got a message but nothing stopped us. I was completely naked by now and he was playing with my breasts as they fell in his face. He was really enjoying it and I gathered that managing sex at all whilst he was drunk was quite unusual (he had whispered to me as much).Suddenly and with no warning the door burst open and his nine friends piled into the room switching on the lights and making one hell of a noise. They all started jeering and laughing and I was totally embarrassed and bloody petrified. I stopped immediately and trying to sound confident I said "Well thanks boys". I grabbed for my dress but couldn't reach and feeling very exposed I spotted a towel on the next bed. Climbing off I made for the towel and wrapping it round me, I quickly assessed my situation.

The rush of adrenaline had sobered me up in one hit. My partner in crime was bemused but said nothing and climbing off the bed and putting on his underpants he lit a cigarette swaggered irritatingly around the room. The jeering continued, they wanted to know if I'd like a threesome or a tensome!? They pulled his leg relentlessly and seemed amazed that he managed to get it up at all. I realised very quickly that I was in a very dangerous situation. They were all drunk and although I hadn't noticed it before I saw evidence on the bedside table that they had been using cocaine. They may be all nice regular guys back in Surrey but they were hammered and drug fuelled and on a

Sex and the Signposts
Gaynor Evans

Stag, where bad behaviour was not only expected it was an essential part of the ritual.

It would seem (much to their annoyance) that their leader was the only one to have got laid. Like a pack of baying wolves with me as their prey, they continued to throw lewd comments in my direction. I managed to grab my dress my knickers and my bag and picking up one shoe I searched around for the other. I asked one of them to help me he made a half hearted attempt but guessing it was under the bed I decided that bending down at this point was not a good idea. The banter got worse and although none of them came in my space I felt very very threatened. My heart was pounding and my mouth was dry and I couldn't think straight.

At this point I decided that attack was the best means of defence and telling them that they could all "Fuck off" I thought sod the shoe and headed for the door. Luck was on my side and they hadn't bothered to shut it and it was wide open. As I walked into the corridor the owner of the orange towel demanded its return. Very chivalrous! He just wanted me to drop it so I would be undressed again. Glaring at him I told him I would leave it at reception. The corridor of the hotel was ridiculously long and reminded me of the one in 'The Shining' well, as horror movies go it would seem I was starring in my own.
As I walked with as much dignity as I could muster down the corridor I heard them calling me back

Sex and the Signposts
Gaynor Evans

"Cinderella Cinderella we have found your shoe". I stopped and turned to see two of them standing in doorway. The nicer of the two guys tossed it along the floor towards me. It fell short and was halfway between me and them. I looked at it on the floor and then saw that the most poisonous of the group, the one who had been the most vocal watching me intently. I knew what he planned. I took one step towards the shoe and he ran like a whippet to get there before me smirking. Calling back over my shoulder "you can keep it" I walked calmly away. As I turned the corner I was relieved to see the ladies I dived inside and caught my breath. My heart was in my mouth and I was shaking. Dropping the towel on the floor along with the one shoe I had escaped with, I quickly pulled the dress over my head, knickers on but no bra, I realised that I had left that behind on the bed. Taking a deep breath, I went out marching swiftly passed reception, barefoot and braless, and out into the night.

The taxi rank was on the same street and grabbing a cab I went back to the apartment. I realized that I had had a lucky escape. What on earth had possessed me to go back to his room? It dawned on me now of course that six beds meant six keys. The door may well have been locked at the start, but it may as well have been wide open. I suppose the others had planned it and must have been listening outside the door waiting for the right moment to burst in. All good fun from a stag night point of view but from mine it was a living nightmare. I had

Sex and the Signposts
Gaynor Evans

been reassured because I had met Rob before and at home. This had lulled me into a false sense of security what an idiot! Thank god I'd used a condom and thank god I had managed to get out quickly. It could have turned really nasty.

I was still visibly shaking as I went through the door to greet the others. They were all waiting for me anxiously, including the charming Spaniard. I gave them details of my ordeal and then making a cup of tea to calm my nerves, I went to bed, laying in the dark going over the events in my mind, I told myself that never again would I be so gullible. I felt stone cold sober, fear is a great leveller.

I told myself reassuringly that at least there had been no harm done. I was safe and sound and had only paid for my stupidity with a pair of shoes and a bra. It could have been so much worse and I wondered if I would ever come across Rob at Ascot, again. Now that could be an interesting encounter, he was certainly no Prince Charming and my glass of champagne might just find its way over his head. In the meantime I fell asleep with the words of the Spanish driver resounding in my ears. I really had been very 'STUPIDO'

Sex and the Signposts
Gaynor Evans

Chapter Twenty Two
CONCLUDING THE COUGAR

So what has the last two years been about? Was it a fifty year old having a temper tantrum...was I acting out my rage because the relationship that I had invested so much time energy and love in had been snatched from me and taken off to Norfolk and was firmly in the hands of another woman. How do you deal with your dreams for the future not only being torn apart but actually been given away to someone else, stolen right from under your nose in fact. It's enough to make the calmest person as mad as hell and I'm not Mrs Placid.

What was I trying to prove with my ongoing dalliances with these fit guys who were young enough to be my sons? I knew I was soothing my battered ego and years of put downs and the insecurity I felt at having been abandoned by someone I thought would always love me and to a degree I suppose I was giving him the finger. (Although I doubt if he could see it in Norfolk) I had come to the conclusion of late that love was overrated didn't last and caused almost as much pain as the joy you feel in the beginning. So was I constantly validating my desirability as a woman every time I succumbed to my desires and bedded one of my boys.? Who knows, but it was intoxicating, full of joy and fun and it made me feel amazing.

Sex and the Signposts
Gaynor Evans

I had my first full sexual experience at the age of seventeen, with my long term boyfriend. I had been scared stiff and was fairly drunk but thought to myself if this was sex I liked it, so the sexual part of me having been awakened became a necessary part of my everyday life. So when you are in a long term relationship sex is on tap available as and when you want it (women usually being the keepers of the sexual allowance) when that ends you find yourself in a sexual desert, you are alone and find yourself wondering where your next sexual encounter is coming from. You miss the physical contact, the intimacy, the joy. So the pheromones rise to the surface and the hunt begins. Providing you follow the rules and hold back on emotional involvement you can play the field have 'Your fix' and move on.

Does that make me sound cynical and hard? Maybe it does but it is only the result of the experiences I have had at the hands of men. I am nobody's victim and I know that I must have played some part in the way things panned out, but my loyalty and faithfulness was never in question. I think I have every right to feel confused by the way things turned out for me. I am proud of the fact that now I was on an even emotional keel and not at the mercy of someone else's behaviour and circumstances. I rarely cried these days (unlike before when I kept Kleenex in business) I apply logic to every situation and always came up with a practical solution rather like my hero Mr. Spock. I have no idea if this is a

Sex and the Signposts
Gaynor Evans

good thing or not but it felt better. I wondered often if I was just burying my feelings deep down and was too scared to tap into them in case I was a molten mess inside. But I feel good and happy and was wallowing quite gratuitously in my new found freedom and loved being in charge of just. me! If I feel like doing something I do it and if that includes making mad passionate love to a twenty year old bring it on! I might sound like silly teenager but what else was there for me?

Should I devote the rest of my life to my family and stay in babysitting getting old and fat and doing charity work? Or the other option that I was constantly questioned about was 'Didn't I want to meet someone' The someone concerned of course would be a nice regular guy of my own age that I could eat out with and watch TV with and do all the coupley things and that actually required me to leave the bedroom. The 'someone' I could take to dinner parties and make everyone round me feel better. They would than feel that they had got it right all along and as a middle-aged woman the only way I was ever going to be truly happy was to be part of a couple.

My ideas of coupling of course were indecent amounts of great and fulfilling sex with totally unsuitable men. No way could I show up with them at a dinner party. But do long term happy marriages really exist? I have a couple of friends of whom this statement is true and I look at them and think yes,

Sex and the Signposts
Gaynor Evans

they have it all. But would that be me, I doubt it my need for excitement and challenge is far too great. This is probably why I married the men I did. They both had a bit of an edge and I think in hindsight I was drawn in because of that rather than settling for someone more ordinary and reliable. So maybe I was destined to fail, but when cupid fires its arrow we are blinded and totally oblivious to men's faults. We imagine that we can smooth off those edges to suit our requirements. Of course this is totally unrealistic but we expect it just the same. I don't have to try and change anything about the toyboys I meet, I accept them as they are and enjoy their optimistic outlook on things, untouched by the trials and tribulations of life for now at at least. They live in the moment and I try and do the same at least whilst I'm with them.

We share some common ground, a high sex drive, a need to quench the never ending thirst created by our hormones. In their case they want to test their sexual prowess on a more worldly audience and one that hopefully will point them in the right direction if they go wrong. In my case I want to feel sexually desired and to be told that I am still attractive and can turn a head or two despite my advancing years.

Surprisingly, I have found their conversation stimulating and interesting and in some cases challenging and there is no expectation on either side. They come back because they want to and I have them back because I love the joy they bring

Sex and the Signposts
Gaynor Evans

me nothing more nothing less. Where there has been a real connection as with Danny it gets harder to keep your emotions under wraps and you form an attachment of sorts. I began to imagine the sort of man he would become and envied the woman that would share his life. At this point you wish you were younger and your mind wanders off to the land of 'What ifs?' I realised that this was a dangerous place to find myself, when he went home after we had spent two consecutive weekends together and I had had the best sex of my life, I was sad and missed him terribly. It dawned on me that this young fledgling had broken through the barrier that I had built around myself and although I was still in control to a degree I was feeling something and it hurt. I reasoned that it was ridiculous and that it would pass but was stupidly elated when he sent me a text a week later saying he was missing me already.

Nevertheless, feelings or not I carried on with the dating game trying to get myself back on track (whatever that was). But it would seem that no matter how old or young you are, you are still susceptible to cupid's arrow and as usual his bloody bow was bent! In any event I had to face the facts and let Danny move on when the time came, hard as it was. But I could not and would not regret the time we had spent together, it had been so uplifting and I wouldn't have missed it.

So, over the last two years I have taken my life by

Sex and the Signposts
Gaynor Evans

the scruff of the neck and given it a good shake. I have experienced great joy in the arms of my boys, some taking me to heaven and back many times and have great affection still for Danny and the Aussie. I have featured in a TV show and appeared in a national newspaper and monthly magazine. I have been lucky enough to be at the birth of both my Grandchildren which I consider an honour and a real life joy. These along with my children family and friends are the important people in my in my life. I retain a wide circle of good and loyal friends who have all tried to support me in my wayward lifestyle and I value them beyond measure.

I have looked death in the face having tried to resuscitate my sister's boyfriend for ten minutes after he suffered a massive and unexpected heart attack. Sadly, he died but, if ever there was a defining moment that was it. You really are a long time dead, you come into the world on your own and so you leave it. Being part of a couple is lovely of course but as most women outlive the man in their lives (unless you marry a younger one) you really do need to retain a sense of self! Life is for living to the fullest extent and I for one intend to continue to slip into old age disgracefully! Now would anyone care to join me?

"The tragedy of old age is not that one is old but that one is young"
Dorian Gray

Sex and the Signposts
Gaynor Evans

PRESENT DAY 2012

Will he actually arrive? He never was on time but my anxiety is rising. I sit opposite Oakwood Station just waiting, checking my phone every ten seconds. When will I come to my senses? It's been so long over eighteen months or more. I had been surprised by his email but very happy he had sought me out again. Suddenly much later than planned, I recognise his familiar outline lumbering up the road. He jumps in the car and kisses me. It's familiar and new all at the same time. With a sigh of relief I drive back to the flat.

It strikes me as I look sideways at him that he looks much younger than I remember. His hair was shorter which always did make him look that way and his clothes were screaming student at me; baggy jeans t-shirt and the obligatory hoodie. I winced inside, asking myself the question of why do I do it? What is it about this man child that keeps him so firmly in my sights my head and once again my heart?

It is indefinable and I can't explain it but within ten minutes of entering the flat we are chatting animatedly listening intently to each other's words and the conversation flows. Our hands and bodies touch here and there and there is a comfortable familiarity to it! His Irish lilting voice soothes my stress away and I laugh at his stories as his deep set green eyes dart this way and that and scan my face

Sex and the Signposts
Gaynor Evans

at regular intervals. He produces chocolates and wine from his bag for me endearing him to me further.

We discuss my family and his and he tells me about his housemates and in between we catch bits of the Olympic opening ceremony. Before long I am curled into him stroking his face and we kiss softly, gentle subtle kisses. I suck bite and nudge his bottom lip and slip my tongue in his mouth and he responds in kind. My stomach melts and I am catapulted into the 'Zone' - This is the place where there will be no resistance, he has kissed away my troubles and I am feeling desired and cherished. Our clothes slip to the floor and the kissing becomes more urgent and I sigh and pull away and looking up at him I say simply "and there it is" he nods at me knowingly understanding me instantly.

His fingers find my inner thighs and he strokes me gently and I inhale sharply as he begins to slide into my panties and into me. I am so excited by now that I am wet with anticipation and as he kneads in and out of me, my juices multiply. Suddenly he withdraws his fingers and raising them to his mouth he licks them I grab his hand and lick them too tasting the familiar saltiness. We stare into each other's eyes and know that we can wait no longer.

I am now naked all except for my bra and kneeling on the carpet resting my head and arms on the sofa he kneels behind me and finding his way he forces

Sex and the Signposts
Gaynor Evans

himself in. I moan as he slides deep inside me, pushing deeper with every thrust. He quickens his pace until I am almost in pain as his penis that is filling every corner of me pounds against my cervix. My legs turn to liquid I am gasping for breath; my whole body is feeling it. He stops suddenly and I realise he is close to orgasm and trying not to. He starts again but unable to stop he comes groaning. He says sorry immediately but I say no need. He has as usual still managed to reduce me to jelly. He helps me to my feet and leading him by the hand I take him to the bedroom 'our' bedroom - The one where we first enjoyed each other's bodies. It has been nearly two years since we have been here.

"My turn" I say smiling and lay on the bed. He knows just what to do and kissing me on the mouth he works his lips down sucking first one nipple then the other and moving slowly over my body, he rests his lips gently, searching for that place that he knows so well. He pushes his tongue in just enough to reach my clitoris and starts licking steadily and hard. I writhe beneath him squeezing up into his mouth. He doesn't move and begins flicking his tongue intensifying his assault on my most sensitive part. I feel the waves begin deep in the pit of my stomach my groans become louder and higher pitched. He is relentless his tongue whipping back and forth, in and out and his body weight is pinning me to the bed as my orgasm rips through my body. I am panting heavily as I come back to earth and he

Sex and the Signposts
Gaynor Evans

gives my clitoris one last and forceful lick and climbs back up kissing me on the mouth and flopping beside me.

We lay side by side bodies touching and I say "Wow" very softly. He smiles and leans over and kisses my shoulder. We lay in silence, feeling no need to speak for a while and then the talking starts again along with more kissing and stroking. Suddenly he is hard again and he swings on top me and finds his way back in. I groan with pleasure and he begins a rhythmic pounding kissing me fast and furiously and I cover his face in small encouraging kisses back. He calls my name as he gets lost in the moment and I whisper softly "I love having you inside me" he replies "I love being inside you". The sexual pleasure gives way to a rush of emotional attachment as I feel so much affection for him. He says nothing but the way he makes love to me touches and reaches me in an inexplicable way. My emotions rush to the surface and right now and in this moment I love him! I fight with myself not to say it out loud. As he continues to move in and out of me and covers me with kisses I hold him tenderly and feel a tear escape and roll down my cheek, I am moved.

Remonstrating with myself internally I know that speaking the love word would not be a good move and so it gets stuck silently in my throat forcing the tears out. I must not let him see, he may not understand. So to distract myself I start moving

Sex and the Signposts
Gaynor Evans

upwards to meet him and draw him further inside me by thrusting my hips hard. He softly whispers that he is coming and I say "yes yes come, come inside me now". I watch his face change as he quietly moans and releases himself into me. I relish the idea of having his fluids inside me for the second time. He clings to me and I stroke his hair and his face and kiss him and he stays inside me for as long as he can knowing how I hate it when he withdraws. When eventually he slips out of me I grimace and he smiles down at me and then begins working his way down my body once again.

I tilt my hips, hands above my head and offer myself in to his mouth. He finds the spot straight away and I'm almost there in seconds. His tongue releases the most massive and intense orgasm from my body I scream and almost lift him off the bed before panting and gasping for breath I allow the pleasure to wash over me.

He lay's beside me kissing me again and I curl in towards him feeling safe secure and absolutely cared for. We fall asleep and during the next few hours we change positions occasionally and kiss in the process. Just before dawn breaks the kissing begins in earnest and we make love for the third time and again I feel an overwhelming love for him as he calls my name.

As I lay in dawn light with him sleeping childlike besides me one arm across my body holding me

Sex and the Signposts
Gaynor Evans

close I again question myself as to why this works so well. Considering the thirty year age gap it seems almost ridiculous. We never do any normal things together like go out or see anyone else. So it is very intense just hours of the two of us talking, making love and occasionally eating. It is not in the real world but then it feels real, special and so uplifting.

We understand each other and the word soul mates comes to mind and although it's a platitude it sort of fits. I know I am slipping into a deep attachment and I must for my own sake try and protect myself. He will be off into the world soon and I will be left behind. I have so many more emotional layers than him he is like a blank canvass and has a long way to grow and feel and be. I know he cares for me but in a way that is abstract and limited but when his guard is down during sex he shows such tenderness and maturity a glimpse of the man to be is evident.

But by the time he fills up his own potential he may look back on our liaison and be embarrassed which I would hate. By then I would be hurtling into old age at an alarming pace. I wonder if I will look back on it and be ashamed. How can something that feels so good and so right be a mistake? I will not allow it to be downgraded. The beauty of it will be that it will never degenerate into fighting and harsh words to lies and deceit to violence and despair. It will remain framed in its bubble forever a surreal relationship that for a moment in time suited us both and ended due to logistics and circumstances and

Sex and the Signposts
Gaynor Evans

not because we grew tired of each other. I must enjoy what time we have together and not over think it.

I'm sure after one of our weekends he leaves smiling feeling relaxed and happy knowing he has fulfilled his brief. I see his confidence grow and I imagine he doesn't waste time analysing it. He probably doesn't think about it much at all until he feels the need to see me again. I am completely at his mercy but somehow I don't care I really don't. It is what it is and I would not have missed it. I feel very lucky to have been so desired, fulfilled and fucked senseless!

By the time I drop him back at the station we will have made love three more times. His energy is boundless. After another long session where he has driven me wild with desire and emotion he comes inside me and then starts working his way down my body. With his tongue and mouth in my favourite place he begins to work his magic. I almost come twice but it's just eluding me and I begin to get desperate for release and very frustrated. I try squeezing everything upward and feel it beginning only to have it fall away again. I stroke his hair to encourage him and then scream out in frustration he stops and looks up at me and I say "sorry you must be tired." He smiles and starts again and I say softly "try slowly, slowly". This time it works, this time it erupts beneath his tongue and goes on and on, wave upon wave surges up and over, it was delicious. I

Sex and the Signposts
Gaynor Evans

cry out incoherently and when he is sure I have finished he comes back up to me and we kiss over and over. He is such a joy.

It is sometime later as we find ourselves in the centre of the room and he holds me and we kiss. He towers above me and I have to reach up to kiss his neck and slowly I reach down and undo his belt and his top button. I can feel through his jeans that he is hard again and I try to unzip him but am foxed by buttons (not so easy!) I eventually push his jeans and pants down and holding his erection in my hand I stroke and play with it. I reach back and pull a chair in behind me and sit down and find I am at just the right height level with his groin and I begin to suck and lick.

He tastes of me and him all mixed together. I flick my tongue over the end of his penis, he moans softly. I take it all in my mouth and out again and run my tongue from one end to the other. I cup his balls in one hand and take all of him in my mouth again being careful not to catch his sensitive skin on my teeth he groans. I release him and get back to my feet and we kiss and I know he is keen to get inside me again. So I kneel on the floor he gets behind me and finds his way in fast.

My tongue has worked well; his erection is so full and hard it feels enormous as he rams it in to me. I am lost in painful pleasure as he enters me over and over. Suddenly he slows down almost taking it out

Sex and the Signposts
Gaynor Evans

and then sliding it firmly back in. He does this a number of times teasing me and I can feel every inch of it as he slides it in again. Suddenly he quickens his pace and his pressure and I am unable to speak and I push back at him meeting his thrusts. He is in so deep my stomach hurts, but still he pushes further and deeper. It's so over- powering that I am delirious with pleasure and totally lost to him.

He whispers that he is coming and I say "yes" and he comes for the sixth time inside me. I collapse, my legs are shaking and my insides have melted. God that was good! He pulls me to my feet and I kiss him and we cuddle enjoying the rush and then it's time to take him back to the station.

He promises to come back soon I don't know if he will. He has to go home and find work but I hope he keeps his promise. I can never have enough of him it would seem. I know that in a day or two my longing for him will begin all over again and I will begin the anxious wait. I should stop this be a grown up end it before it ends me. But I can't I'm in too deep and as I said completely at his mercy. It will all end in tears and all of the tears will be mine. I ask myself yet again - is the joy I just experienced worth the risk? I smile as I answer myself bloody hell **Yes**!!

'For those who have experienced the joy, no explanation is necessary. For those who haven't no explanation is possible'

Sex and the Signposts
Gaynor Evans

Made in the USA
Charleston, SC
07 September 2013